# REDISCOVERING THE CHARACTER OF MANHOOD

## A Young Man's Guide to Building Integrity

## Greg S. Baker

*For Christian Boys, Teens, Young Men, and Dads*

# Rediscovering the Character of Manhood

A Young Man's Guide to Building Integrity
For Christian Boys, Teens, Young Men, and Dads

by

Greg S. Baker

Independently Published

Copyright © 2018

ISBN: 9781726700122

First Edition

All Scripture quotations are from the King James Bible.

# Other Books by Greg S. Baker

## Christian and Christian Living

*Fitly Spoken – Developing Effective Communication and Social Skills*

*Restoring a Fallen Christian – Rebuilding Lives for the Cause of Christ*

*The Great Tribulation and the Day of the Lord: Reconciling the Premillennial Approach to Revelation*

*The Gospel of Manhood According to Dad – A Young Man's Guide to Becoming a Man*

*Rediscovering the Character of Manhood – A Young Man's Guide to Building Integrity*

*Stressin' Over Stress – Six Ways to Handle Stress*

## Biblical Fiction Novels

The Davidic Chronicles

Book One - *Anointed*

Book Two - *Valiant*

Book Three – *Fugitive*

More to come…

## Young Adult Adventure Novels

Isle of the Phoenix Novels

*The Phoenix Quest*

*In the Dragon's Shadow*

More to come…

www.GregSBaker.com

# Disclaimer

The stories in this book are as I recall them. My memory over the years has undoubtedly transposed some of them into an exaggeration of some kind or another, and if other participants in these stories were asked about the same events, they may very well remember them differently.

However, it is my perspective on these events that has helped shape my life into the man I am today. I will recount them as accurately as I can recall them, but I make no claim that they happened exactly as I describe—only as I remember them. I am fully aware that immaturity and/or emotions of the time can skew the memories I have from the literal truth, and we tend to remember only the parts that make the greatest impact on our lives. It was, however, those parts that helped shape the man I became.

*Except for immediate family, all names have been changed to protect identities.*

# My Hope for This Book

Becoming a man in an everchanging landscape has always been challenging. A boy must navigate the intricacies of life in a world where technology and permissiveness have become enablers of all kinds of behavior and then emerge into adulthood as a man whom any father or mother would be proud of. That process is not easy. Defining manhood nowadays is different than it once was. Society is challenging traditional definitions and thereby challenges the values behind those definitions. This book seeks to make clear the muddy waters of growing up and give dads and boys the insight needed to help boys become the men God means for them to become.

I grew up in a traditional, Christian family. I am a second-generation Christian. I never used drugs. I never smoked. I never drank alcohol. I never cussed. I was a virgin when I got married. And I pastored a church for thirteen years. I am now the father of four sons of my own. For the Christian parents trying to rear their sons in a Christian home, this book is for you and for your sons. The stories in this book are normal, everyday encounters of growing up and becoming a man. It can be an invaluable tool to help guide your son into adulthood.

My hope is that you will take this book, dad, and read through it with your son. More importantly though, let the stories you read spark your own memories—memories you can share with your son of your own journey into manhood. Your stories will have the greatest impact on your boys.

# Dedication

For my two youngest sons, Owen and Jacen. You both have taught me so much—even about manhood. I love you both!

# Acknowledgments

A book like this that is based on so much of my own life means there are too many people to appropriately thank. My parents, of course, deserve the most credit. They, after all, introduced me to manhood and to a relationship with Jesus Christ.

In a general way, I want to thank every person who is mentioned in this book. For the most part, their names have been changed in this writing, but their influence on my life, big and little, positive and negative, have shaped me into the man I am. These are the people who make up my life, for life is relationships, and there is value and weight to every person. They all matter.

Thank you.

# Table of Contents

# Introduction to the Character of Manhood

**M**anhood is about the little things of life. Trauma, heavy burdens, and extreme situations are not what makes a man. A man's character may be revealed in times like that, but the little things learned along the way are what builds a man's character and allows him to carry the heavy loads of life.

Twenty-three times in Proverbs, the phrase, "My son," appears. Proverbs is a father's attempt to teach his son about the little things in life so that his son would be capable of handling the weightier matters he would eventually face as king of one of the most powerful and influential nations in the world at that time.

Solomon wanted to pass on to his son the lessons he had learned. He wanted to teach his son what character and integrity meant. He wanted his son to grow up into a man of decency, honor, integrity, honesty, and godliness. Being a man isn't about how tough you are, how much pain you can endure, how well you can dominate someone physically, or how skilled you are at a sport or even a trade. You will find none of those areas addressed in the advice Solomon gave to his son in the book of Proverbs.

We tend to look at Esau and say he was a man's man, but Jacob was a momma's boy. Neither was true, and neither exhibited true qualities of manhood. In fact, if you examine Jacob's deeds after he left home, he did many things that we would consider manly, but at that time of his life, I wouldn't give you a nickel for his manhood—or Esau's. Jesus was a man, and He let the disciple John lean against His breast (John 13:35), and that gesture was not an act of feminism, being gay, or being weak. Yet our Christian society never points to that example as one of manliness! But I dare say that both Jesus and John were incredibly strong men who understood manhood.

This is the dilemma that fathers face. How do we bring our boys into manhood in a world where manhood is often confused with gladiator-style attributes? We want our boys to be men, and well we should, but manhood isn't about the ability to take a hit in football, but rather, it's how he conducts himself on the field and his attitude toward his opponent. Doing your best and playing your hardest is not the same as thinking of ways to hurt your opponents or losing your temper when you think the other team cheated. I'd rather have a boy who knows how to control his temper than one that knows how to win a ballgame.

This book is about the challenges a boy must face to navigate the normal, everyday situations of life—girls, school, church, family, and friends. The stories in this book are not of death-defying situations, gang involvement, prison, or deep sin. For the most part, they are about what your son may face growing up in the United States in a Christian home.

Dad, start in any chapter you think is most needful to your son. Read it with him, for I am hoping it will inspire you to share your own stories of growing up and help you add your own lessons as you guide your son to manhood.

This book is what every father would want to say to his son, but just may not know how.

# CHAPTER ONE
# Cheaters Are Cowards

Somehow and in some way, society has accepted cheating as a legitimate way to get ahead. The practice has become so common that I've even heard people use the excuse, "But everyone's doing it," as justification for cheating. Indeed, I heard an eighth grader say, "Cheating is only wrong if you get caught." As a result of these philosophies and others like them, teenagers are seemingly growing up with a belief that right and wrong are relative. I sometimes corner teenagers and teasingly demand, "Have you cheated in school this year?" Sheepishly, 90 percent of them admit that they have—and these are Christian kids!

Two prevailing philosophies seem to dominate our thinking when it comes to things like cheating, lying, and other so-called benign sins:

1. It's only wrong if you get caught.
2. As long as you don't hurt someone else, then it's not wrong.

These philosophies and others like them have undermined character and integrity more than anything else. These dangerous values—and yes, they are a type of value—have created an atmosphere of distrust and immaturity.

But cheating is stealing. Plain and simple.

When you cheat, you steal someone else's work while perpetuating the lie that you know something or accomplished something you did not. Cheating is wrong, and worse, it inhibits maturity and the growth of your character. Maturity is the ability to take responsibility for your responsibilities, and cheating is the direct antithesis of taking responsibility. Cheating attempts to sidestep responsibility—both the work involved in fulfilling the responsibility and the consequences for failing to fulfill the responsibility. In effect, cheating is the coward's way out.

Yes, cheaters are cowards. They dare not face their own laziness, their own immaturity, those who counted on them, and the consequences of their laziness. Becoming a man means owning up to your mistakes and your faults. Only cowards seek to evade the consequences of their own actions, but a real man faces up to them.

Son, don't be a coward.

## The Cheater

I don't recall kindergarten, but I do remember several things from first grade. I attended a school in Phoenix called Nevitt Elementary, located not far from my house on Lynne Lane. This was back in the day when, even as a first grader, I walked to and from school by myself or with a friend—oh, I'm sure Mom came along a time or two as well.

My first-grade teacher was Mrs. Ringer. Her classroom was set up with the desks in a horseshoe shape that faced a giant chalkboard against the wall at the top of the U. In 1981 and to a small first grader, that chalkboard looked enormous. My fingers itched to get my hands on a piece of chalk and draw on that huge, green canvas. Do you know how many bombers I could draw and how many cities I could destroy on such a large work area? My little imagination saw so many possibilities, and I wanted that chalkboard all to myself.

I only had one problem to overcome. In order to draw on the chalkboard, we had to get our work done. That was great—if you were the first person done, for then you'd have the entire chalkboard to yourself. But as other kids finished, the chalkboard became more crowded, leaving less room to draw.

What I needed was an edge—some way to get my work done in a hurry and get to the chalkboard before anyone else. I found the solution in Nova, the girl sitting next to me. Nova was a spindly girl, not very popular, and not at all interested in the chalkboard—which played right into my devious first-grade brain. She was also a fast worker who usually finished her work well ahead of me. She had one other attribute that helped me conceive of a thoroughly daring plan—at least for me. She had to go to the bathroom—frequently.

Mrs. Ringer handed out a worksheet to all the kids and told us to get to work on it. And as for her usual reward, she told us that as soon as we finished, we could draw on the chalkboard. Nova, of course, got to work right away. I procrastinated, knowing that I wouldn't need to do the work if my plan came together. Sure enough, Nova was nearly finished—well ahead of all the other kids—when she had to use the bathroom.

I watched Nova slip out of her chair and head off to get permission. No sooner did she get around the desks and near the teacher when I swapped papers with her. Hurriedly, I erased her name at the top and wrote mine over it. And then writing her name on my paper, I put it on her desk. I hastily finished the tiny portion she had not yet done and then stood up, finished paper in hand.

All the kids looked up, obviously surprised that I'd finished my work so quickly. Proudly, I walked around the perimeter of the desks to Mrs. Ringer's desk and placed Nova's work in the designated tray.

"Done already, Gregory?" Mrs. Ringer asked, her eyebrows rising slightly in surprise.

"Yes, Ma'am," I replied politely, just as my mother had taught me. "May I draw on the chalkboard?"

"If you've done your work, you can." She glanced at the paper in the tray to make sure it was complete and then looked back down at whatever it was she was doing.

I took that dismissal as permission. Extremely pleased that my plan had worked so well, I ran over to the chalkboard and immediately claimed the longest and best piece of chalk available. I had the entire chalkboard to myself with oodles and oodles of space to draw bombers, space aliens, alien ships, and thermonuclear explosions—all of which quite naturally went together in my little brain.

I got to work—or playing.

Not long after, I dimly remember Nova's returning to the classroom and making her way to her desk. By this time, I was well on my way to depicting the destruction of the entire world and was so engrossed in my masterpiece that I only distantly realized that Nova had begun to cry. Besides, my job wasn't to console her or even to figure out what was wrong with her. That was the teacher's job, so I kept drawing.

Mrs. Ringer got up from her desk and walked over to Nova. A moment later, Mrs. Ringer stalked back and picked up my paper from the tray on her desk. I continued drawing, completely engrossed in my art.

The first indication I had that my plan was unraveling was when my teacher grabbed my arm and pulled me back toward my desk. I didn't resist, and I don't even know what happened to the chalk I held. The next thing I knew, I stood before a teary-eyed Nova, and Mrs. Ringer was shoving my stolen work under my nose.

"Is this your paper, Gregory?" she demanded. Her stern tone of voice along with the fact that she still had a death grip on my arm alerted me that I was probably in big trouble.

I decided to stall. "It's got my name on it," I protested.

"This name? Here?" She stabbed a finger at the top of the paper.

And then I saw it—the one great fault of my master plan. My name was clearly visible there, all right, but right beneath it, not completely erased was Nova's name. I'd failed to take into account that first graders tend to write rather hard. Erasing her name hadn't really done the trick as I had intended.

I looked up and found Nova's eyes. All girls were ugly to me at that age, but I couldn't help but notice the hurt and torment in her eyes. I was very young, and I didn't fully understand what I had done or how much I had hurt Nova. I did understand that I had done wrong, and I certainly understood my teacher's intentions when she started pulling me toward the door.

"I think you need to visit the principal, young man," she said. A worse threat she could not have given me. I didn't even know who the principal was! I'm sure I'd seen him or her, but the principal was a kid-eating monster who terrified little boys and girls. I'd never been to the principal's office. I'm not even sure I knew where it was!

Terrified now, I started crying as soon as we got out the door. I heard the heavy door slam shut, and we stood on the sidewalk outside. Tears streamed down my face. Getting to draw on the chalkboard early certainly wasn't worth being dragged to the principal's office.

Mrs. Ringer, God bless her, had pity on me. Perhaps because I'd never been in trouble before or maybe she sensed true remorse—and no, I didn't feel bad because I'd hurt Nova. I felt bad because I had been caught, and I didn't want to face up to the consequences. My cowardly little heart trembled at the thought of having to see the principal.

Turning to me, Mrs. Ringer put on her best glare. "You know what you did was wrong, right?"

That last part of her question was a bit confusing, but I dared not seek clarification, so I just nodded and muttered, "Yes, Ma'am."

"You really hurt Nova, you know. She didn't deserve to have her work stolen. Do you understand?"

No, not really, but again, I nodded. "Yes, Ma'am."

"Cheating is wrong, Gregory. Promise me you won't do it again."

I nodded vigorously—anything to get out of having to see the principal. "I promise."

"But you're still in trouble, Gregory. You're going to have to stay after class."

Well, that was a sight better than having to face the principal, so I counted my blessings, so to speak. She marched me back into class, sat me down, erased my name from Nova's paper, and wrote Nova's back on her paper. She then erased Nova's name from my answerless paper and wrote mine in the appropriate place.

"Now get to work, Greg," she ordered.

I gulped and got to work. I dared not look up. For some reason, I didn't want to see Nova's eyes again.

At the end of the day, Mrs. Ringer had all the kids stand and put their chairs on top of their desks—except for me. I sat in my chair while all the other kids lined up to leave and the lights were turned off. By this time, things had settled down a bit in my mind, and I was a bit peeved. I'm not exactly sure at what—me, Nova, or being caught. Regardless, when Mrs. Ringer took pity on me once again and told me I could get in line to go home, I felt cheated. I folded my arms and scrunched down in my chair, trying to blend in with the near darkness. I'd been caught. This was my punishment. How dare she take that away!

Looking back, I feel my reaction at the last was peculiar to say the least. Perhaps I felt that if I had been punished in that way, then I wouldn't meet any other—or worse—punishment later. I'm not exactly sure what made me decide I'd been cheated of my punishment, but I have certainly never forgotten that day or Nova's eyes.

I learned a valuable lesson the day I stole Nova's paper the hard way. Cheating is stealing, and cheaters are certainly cowards.

## Revenge of the Cheated

During my junior year in high school, I got to be on the other side of the cheating experience. While taking a science test—can't remember which particular branch of science—I happened to notice the kid next to me surreptitiously glancing over at my paper and copying my answers. We hadn't gotten far into the test, so clearly, he had done nothing to prepare for the exam.

When I noticed his cheating off my work, I got angry. It struck me that I had put a lot of effort into preparing to take that test, so why should he steal my answers—essentially stealing my work, so to speak? It wasn't right, and he hadn't even asked me if he could cheat off my work!

My conniving brain hit upon a plan. I began writing down just slightly wrong answers to each question. Nothing significant, mind you, but wrong enough that our teacher would have to mark each one wrong if turned in like that. For the entire test, he copied every one of my incorrect answers.

Finished, I leaned back and began looking over my work as if I were double-checking the answers. Impatient, he got up and turned in his test. When he returned to his seat, he found me hard at work erasing all my answers and writing in the correct ones. I felt him staring at me, clearly unsure what to think about my peculiar behavior.

I pretended not to notice.

The next day, when we received our tests back, I got an A, but he got a flat F. I caught him looking over at my test result, then back at his, and then back at mine. He finally raised his eyes to meet mine. "Yes?" I asked, all innocent like.

His eyes tightened and his cheeks flushed a bit, but he hurriedly looked away, muttering, "Nothin'."

I then had the gall to ask, "How'd you do on the test?"

He flipped it over so I couldn't see the large F circled on top of his paper. He muttered something I didn't catch. He clearly wanted to confront me about the grade, obviously suspicious that I had somehow caused him to receive a bad grade. Having attempted to cheat off me, he knew he didn't have the moral ground to confront me. There is no stopping a man who knows he's in the right, but a man who knows he is in the wrong will perform cowardly acts to hide it.

So having had my revenge on him for attempting to cheat off me, I was satisfied with the results and let the matter go. Perhaps I shouldn't have taken such perverse joy in seeing him get an F on that test, but I had felt like he was attempting to steal from me. He was.

Cheating is stealing, and cowards cheat. He was looking for the easy way out of the fact that he had not studied for the test. He didn't want to face the consequences of his own laziness. In the end, his attempted theft left him with no moral position to face me. What could he say? "You cheated me out of cheating you! How dare you!" No, even in his own mind, he could see the stupidity of saying something like that.

Son, are you a cheater? Have you tried to get ahead on the work and effort of someone else? Cheaters are cowards, so what type of man are you?

# CHAPTER TWO
# The Truth of Lies

Sin has created a world where gray exists. God is clear cut black and white. But within a sinful world, gray exists. In my opinion, the greatest mark of our sin-cursed world is that each Christian will invariably find himself in a position where doing wrong will seem like the right thing to do—or at least the lesser of two evils.

For example, how many of us will tell a "white" lie to save someone's feelings? I dare say that everyone will. If you lived in Nazi Germany and were harboring Jews in your basement, would you lie to the Gestapo to keep the Jews safe? Of course you would. In the Bible, Rahab the harlot lied to her king about the whereabouts of the Israelite spies. I mean she flat out lied, with a straight face.[1] She saved the spies' lives with her lie and was rewarded by being spared when Jericho was eventually conquered by Joshua.[2] Was she right to do so? Was her lie a sin? That is the problem with a sin-cursed world. In a totally righteous world, her lies would have never even been necessary.

---

[1] Joshua 2:3-6.
[2] Joshua 6:23.

If a lie is a sin and Satan is the father of all lies,[3] then once again, we fall victim to this sinful world whenever we fall into that gray zone of the lesser of two evils. It is one of the great tragedies of sin. A man must deal with this gray zone. I think it is safe to say that a man—a real man—should be truthful and honest. A boy or a teenager who cannot tell the truth is no real man, and he becomes a coward because he is unable to face the truth.

Why do we lie? I believe there are several reasons:

1. To get something we think we can only get through a lie
2. To avoid the consequences of our actions
3. To avoid difficult or awkward situations
4. To right a perceived wrong

The fourth reason may seem strange, but many people will lie as their only way to right some perceived wrong done to them. In this case, it is "the-end-justifies-the-means" mentality. Politicians exploit the fourth reason all the time. They believe strongly that a particular candidate, if elected, would do a great deal of harm in office, so to prevent what they see as a tragedy, they will lie and cheat to keep that person from being elected. To them, their lies are helping people and preventing a greater wrong. They feel no guilt or remorse for their dishonesty.

Lying is wrong, and a true man will stand up for the truth and tell the truth. I fully understand that a man will face those gray areas already mentioned, but the character of a truthful man will best know how to deal with such situations. Without a truthful

---

[3] John 8:44.

character, a man will rely upon the lies to deliver him from trouble instead of the truth.

## The Revenge of a Liar's Mother

I had a lying problem when growing up. I lied even when the truth would have been easier. My lying became habitual, moving to the point where I developed a mischievous mind.[4] I must have been about twelve or thirteen years old when I wandered into my brother Kevin's room and spotted a twenty-dollar bill lying on his dresser. I looked carefully around and upon determining that I could steal the money without being caught, I snatched it and walked out.

Now the fact that I suddenly had twenty dollars and my brother was missing twenty dollars would look mighty suspicious, so I hatched a story I felt fairly sure would be believable enough without being able to be verified either way.

You see, a good lie must have enough plausible truth in it to make it believable. Satan did the same thing with Eve when he deceived her.[5] He mixed a lie in with the truth so that it would be believable enough to deceive. I didn't need my parents or my brother to completely believe me. I only needed them to have enough doubt about the lie that they couldn't absolutely prove that I had stolen my brother's money.

So at my next soccer practice, I put my carefully crafted story into play. Following the conclusion of the practice, I crumpled up the bill so that it wouldn't resemble the more pristine bill that was missing from my brother's room. Then when no one was looking,

---

[4] Proverbs 6:28, 10:23, 12:21, 17:20; Ecclesiastes 10:13.
[5] Genesis 3:1-7.

I tossed the bill onto the ground between the soccer field and where the cars were parked.

The next part of the plan had to work perfectly. Making sure I had witnesses, I bent down and picked up the crumpled bill. "Hey! Look what I found," I said loud enough for those nearby to hear. I flattened the bill and looked suitably surprised at having "found" a $20 bill. I rushed over to the car where my mom waited to pick me up and flourished the bill for her to see. "Look what I found, Mom!"

Mom looked hard at me, hardly even glancing at the $20 bill. She said nothing which I thought was ominous, but at the same time, I felt relieved. She hadn't questioned my find, and it looked as if I would get away with my lie and theft. The mischievous mind loves the superior feeling of having gotten away with something. The Bible warns against this mentality and of its dangers, but getting away with something, for me and at that age, made me feel superior and smarter than my mother.

What I didn't know was that she was fully aware of my theft and my lie. Since I had arranged things in such a way that she could not prove it, she decided to pursue a different route of getting to the truth—one I am convinced nearly killed me. The mother of a liar, particularly a Christian mother, can appeal to a Higher Court.

The following Sunday, we all went to church again. My brother had discovered the missing $20 and had predictably accused me of the theft, but since I had "witnesses" who could testify that I found $20 after a soccer practice, I left him fuming ineffectively while I retained the money. I felt quite pleased with myself and with the success of my plan. So to be very blunt about it, I sat through the entire church service without feeling an ounce of guilt. I had won. I had gotten away with it. I was smarter than them all!

At the conclusion of the service, our pastor opened an invitation to the front altar for people to do business with God. My mother slipped out and went forward, but I sat comfortably in my seat, waiting for the service to end so I could plot what I'd do with my ill-gotten gains. What I didn't know was the reason why my mother had gone to the altar to pray.

My mother went to the front, knelt down, and began to pray, "Father, I need some help with my son. I know he stole that money, and I know he's lying about how he got it. Do whatever You need to do to get him to admit his wrong."

That was a scary prayer. When a mother gives God a blank check to do whatever God wants to do to an unrepentant, mischievous thief and liar who also happened to be her son, you know she's serious. In the Bible, God had always been particularly attentive to the prayers of a mother. Cutting God loose like that…well, it could be scary. For me, the results were terrifying.

Back in my seat, I began to fidget. A pressure unlike anything I'd ever felt in my entire life began to descend upon me. I felt like something was driving me into the pew where I sat. The weight of that "something" was both real and intangible at the same time. The pressure seemed to center on my mind and my thoughts, but every muscle in my body tensed as if trying to hold up a great weight. The pressure increased to the point where I literally thought I was going to die. My heart felt as if a hand had grabbed it and began to squeeze. My head felt ready to explode.

A single thought rose to my conscious mind: *I stole my brother's money.*

As if God had taken a branding iron and seared the truth of what I had done in my brain, I could only think of that one thing. Unless I did something about it, I believed I would die. The moment I determined to get it right, my body was freed.

I jumped up out of the seat and rushed down the center aisle and met my mom coming back. I grabbed her, sobbing uncontrollably. Unable to get the words out right, I blurted, "I took it! I took the money!"

Mom took my arms and pushed me back away from her. With a stern and totally unsympathetic look, she said, "I know." She then left me standing there in the middle of the aisle with the entire church looking at me...and I was still crying.

That incident pretty much cured me of stealing—and lying.

I'll never forget that experience and the utter disappointment on my mother's face that she had to pray such an alarming prayer. But my mother was no longer willing to tolerate a son who could so easily steal and lie and then not be bothered by his sin. My shamelessness bothered her most of all. My blatant disregard for her and my brother as well as my complete lack of guilt over what I'd done had driven my mother to a point where she had willingly unleashed God's wrath upon me.

I didn't even know mothers could do that!

Perhaps the most alarming aspect in a boy or a young man is not feeling guilty for doing wrong. No boy should grow up thinking that getting away with mischief is good. I learned the hard way, and I had much repenting and retraining of my mind ahead of me before I could be in a place where I felt clean again. But the trip out of the dirty pit of my own mind was totally worth it.

Son, are you a liar? Do you use lies to get out of trouble? What do you need to do to make it right?

# CHAPTER THREE
# Knowing What You Stand For

A real man stands for something greater than himself. This is one of the keys to manhood. When the only thing you stand for is yourself, then you become the totality of your own reality and can see nothing without first running it through the filter of your own needs, wants, and desires. This is a narrow landscape at best and a deadly trap at worst.

The average man sees life through a narrow range of insight. It could be selfishness, greed, lust, fame, or even something noble, like fitness, intelligence, knowledge, or respect. These choices, however, limit a man. They bind him to a misunderstanding of life and purpose, affecting every single relationship he has.

Acts 8 tells of a man named Simon who witnessed the power of the apostles' ability to grant the Holy Ghost through the laying on of hands. He had become a believer in Jesus and had even followed the apostles around, learning from them and watching them. By all outward appearances, he was a growing Christian.

However, a request he made to Peter revealed his true thought process. He demanded, "Give me also this power, that on whomsoever I lay hands, he may receive the Holy Ghost."[6] If you notice, he didn't ask what he would need to do to acquire this power; he offered to purchase it.

In Simon's mind, apparently, everything was for sale. This was his worldview. This is how he did business and interacted with his relationships. It all centered around him.

Peter's response was harsh: "Thy money perish with thee, because thou hast thought that the gift of God may be purchased with money. Thou hast neither part nor lot in this matter: for thy heart is not right in the sight of God. Repent therefore of this thy wickedness, and pray God, if perhaps the thought of thine heart may be forgiven thee. For I perceive that thou art in the gall of bitterness, and in the bond of iniquity."[7]

Peter saw right to the heart of the problem. Simon's worldview and outlook on life stemmed from a self-centered perspective, which had created a trap into which he had fallen. The trap of his own making bound him both mentally and emotionally. This is often the result when a man does not stand up for something that is greater than himself.

I wrote the following short story to illustrate this truth. It is both an interesting story and one that is also packed full of interesting lessons.

## The Hero Coward – A Civil War Tale of Ironic Tragedy

Patrick Nolan didn't think of himself as a coward. But when a Union musket ball bit into the tree next to his head, sending little

---

[6] Acts 8:19.
[7] Acts 8:20-23.

pieces of wood into his ear and scalp, Patrick lost all thought of anything except one: get away!

His rifle fell from nerveless fingers, and his eyes locked on the looming, angry, ugly faces of the Union soldiers scrambling toward him with deadly intent. Losing all sense of reality and thought, except one, he darted down the back slope of the forested ridge that his brigade had just charged up. Bullets and musket balls whipped through the trees, sounding like angry bees or splatting sickeningly against tree trunks. The screams of men locked in battle relentlessly followed him as he plunged downward, seeking safety.

Tree branches tugged at his clothes, snagging and resisting his efforts to flee. He tripped on a root and went sprawling, his shoulder slamming hard into the base of an oak tree and sending waves of pain down his spine. The bullets began to fall closer, zipping and snapping through the underbrush, punching small holes in leaves and sending wooden shrapnel flying through the air every time one hit a tree.

Patrick lay paralyzed. He couldn't think. He didn't know how to get away. Confederate soldiers rushed past him, struggling uphill toward the crest of the ridge where the Yanks now poured over, whooping, screaming, and shouting profanities at their Rebel brothers.

One thin boy, his first stubble of a beard just appearing on his pale face, pitched over and fell not a foot from where Patrick lay. Where his eye should have been, a bloody hole was now visible. The sight was too much for Patrick. In his wildest dreams, he never envisioned battle to be like this. He had joined for the adventure the recruiter had promised and to set right the Northern wrongs. This wasn't an adventure, and nothing would ever be put right this way. This was pure death! His fear paralyzed him beyond the ability to move; his mind found the only available escape—he fainted.

Patrick had no idea how long he lay unconscious under the oak tree, but when his eyes finally fluttered open, the sun had slipped down behind the ridge shading everything in deep shadows. He heard nothing. Even the birds had forsaken this part of the forest as if the battle waged here had laid a curse of death on it, and life would be an unwelcomed intrusion.

His heart pounding, he inched his head up and peered around. Nothing. Not a sign of life. Slowly, he rose to his feet, ignoring his throbbing shoulder, and took a deep breath, trying to figure out what to do.

From what he could see, it looked as if the Union soldiers had overrun the Confederate position here. Bodies from both armies lay sprawled in grotesque positions. Abandoned equipment littered the ridge, but strangely, the horse trail that ran parallel to the ridge and along the bottom of the ravine seemed free of the carnage. The battle had moved elsewhere. He was alone.

Patrick abruptly decided on what he needed to do. If he was now behind enemy lines, being caught in a Confederate uniform would spell his death for sure. These Yanks under General Grant took no quarter, he had heard. They were raging, uncontrollable barbarians. He hurried over to the first dead Union solider he could find and began to strip the man of his uniform.

"Surin you won't be needin' it, anyhow," he muttered as he worked. He would have to get back to Georgia somehow. *Yes sir, Patrick Nolan didn't belong in any war, no how!* he thought bitterly. *What did Jefferson Davis ever do for me, anyway?*

Patrick had no idea what regiment the Union soldier had been part of. His own commander, A. P. Hill, had dragged the

Confederate Third Corps to this wilderness to blunt General Grant's advance into Virginia. Patrick bitterly regretted not deserting earlier—not that he believed himself to be a coward. He simply didn't belong in this stupid war. "I ain't no coward!" he growled to himself, yanking off the corpse's trousers. "This ain't my war."

He had just finished pulling on the Yank's trousers when the muffled sound of a body of horses rushing along the trail at the bottom of the hill froze his blood. He paused in his efforts to undo the dead Yank's jacket. He bit down on his lip hard enough to draw blood and prayed to God that the cavalry unit was in too much of a rush to notice him sitting on the side of the ridge. He didn't really care which side they were on. He only wanted to get away—back to Georgia where he belonged.

He had no such luck.

"Lieutenant!" the lead rider yelled, pulling his horse to a sliding halt and pointing directly at Patrick. "Look yonder!"

The lieutenant, a tall gangly man with a thick beard that looked much too large for such a skinny face, peered at Patrick. Only then did Patrick notice the blue uniforms. He bolted.

"He's runnin'!" someone yelled. "Get 'em!" A bullet zipped by Patrick's head and splattered against a trunk a few yards ahead. All thought fled from Nolan's mind. He ran blindly, not even realizing that he fled down the easiest path for the Union horses to take—the trail at the bottom of the ravine.

He ran, and a few more shots buzzed angrily by him. He could feel the ground shaking as the horses pounded after him. "A spy!" someone yelled. Patrick pushed on even faster until a slug caught him in the leg. His suddenly uncooperative leg launched him into a flailing roll over the narrow trail.

He groaned, clutching at his leg and rolling from side to side in a vain effort to control the agony. The Union cavalry rode up and surrounded him. Patrick closed his eyes and began to tremble violently, expecting a bullet to end his life at any moment.

"Surin a spy, Lieutenant. Look at them trousers."

"He took it off of one of ours," someone else concurred. "I seen him. What you think? He a spy?"

A chorus of laughing agreements followed. "Get a rope," Patrick heard to his horror.

Patrick's eyes snapped open in panic. Forgetting the pain, he tried to scramble up the slope of the ridge, confused as to why his leg would not obey him. "Not a spy!" he yelled. "Not a spy!"

"Shut yer blabberin'," one yelled, dismounting. He grabbed Patrick by his injured leg and jerked him back down onto the trail. Agony rolled over him, and all his strength abandoned him at the same time. "Where you from?" his tormentor demanded.

"F-f-from? I—I'm..."

"He's a spy," the lieutenant interrupted confidently. "Get the rope."

"No!" Panic took over again, but Patrick had nowhere to go. The men laughed and kicked him, while another took down a rope and cast about for a stout limb to toss it over.

That's when the Confederate cavalry swept in, whooping, and hollering the famous Rebel yell. The first volley cut three of the Union boys right out of their saddles.

"Rebels!" shouted the Union lieutenant. Those were his last words as a passing scar-faced Confederate officer chopped at him with a saber.

Patrick closed his eyes in terror once more. He wished he could run, but the noise of the battle froze him in place. It soon stopped however, and Patrick slowly came to realize a different group of men had surrounded him. He opened his eyes to see gray uniformed men peering down at him.

"Who're you?" demanded a blurry man wearing a Confederate captain's insignia. The man's viciously scared face held no sympathy.

"Nolan," Patrick managed to squeak out, feeling a bit more hopeful of being rescued by men from the South.

"He's wearin' a Confederate coat," a red-faced man pointed out. "and Yank trousers."

"A spy?" Scarface asked, rubbing his chin.

Patrick's heart turned to stone. He wanted to protest, to deny it, to explain what had happened, but a deserter was hung as quickly as a spy these days. Another of the soldiers interrupted. "Cap, looky at these here papers!"

The other soldier had been rummaging through the saddle bags of the milling Union horses and had discovered some interesting dispatches in the Union lieutenant's bags. The captain grabbed the papers and flipped through them, scowling the entire time. Finally, he looked up and settled a glare on Patrick. "They were protecting you, weren't they?" He waved the papers at Nolan. "These are drawings of our defenses! You brought them! You're a spy!"

"No!" Patrick managed to yell.

"Get a rope!"

Patrick couldn't protest. He couldn't even resist. Fear so consumed him that he didn't even struggle as they hung him. Nolan's last thought was: *I'm not a coward! I'm not!*

The deed done, the Confederates stared at the swinging body until the legs stopped kicking. The captain then snorted in disgust and pulled out a knife. "Get that coat off him. No sense despoiling it any more than it is. I got a message to send them Yanks."

Sometime later, a strong Union patrol led by Colonel Miles rode up the abandoned trail and discovered a body hanging from a high tree branch. Miles eyed the body in speculation. The man wore Union trousers, no coat or shirt, and had the words "Yank Spy" carved gruesomely into his chest. A wad of papers had been jammed into the dead man's open mouth, and his eyes bugled from a malnourished face.

"What do you make of it?" his aide asked, not really liking the too-common sight of a hung man these days.

"Looks like one of ours tried to make it back to us, and his luck ran out. God have mercy on him." Miles sighed deeply. "Cut him down. Try to find a name if you can—though I doubt you will. We'll bury him in a proper Union uniform with a medal pinned to his chest."

"A medal, sir?"

"Yes. He died a hero for the Union. We'll give him a hero's burial."

## Standing Tall on Flat Tires

When my wife Liberty and I were first married, we moved into an upstairs apartment in downtown Hammond, Indiana. The apartment was one of four in a large renovated house that had once been built in a prestigious part of town that had long since gone downhill. I'd done my research into the neighborhood, however, even knocking on every door on the street and meeting the neighbors before signing the lease. The problem wasn't with those neighbors, but with the people my landlord allowed to move into the other apartments in our building.

One such renter was a man who didn't actually belong there. He just moved in after his girlfriend had rented the place. He lived directly underneath my apartment, and he seemed nice enough when I first met him, but he had a problem. He smoked marijuana.

I'm fairly naïve about things like that, and the only other time I'd ever smelled marijuana was while inviting people to church as a teenager with an older man from our church. After we left a particular house, he said, "Do you know what that smell was?" I didn't and said so. "That's marijuana," he explained.

The ventilation of the apartment wasn't the greatest, and whatever he was doing downstairs filled our little upstairs apartment with an odor I'd only ever smelled one time before. "That's marijuana," I told my wife.

We were only a few months married, so I'm sure she didn't know what I was going to do. Neither did I. My fear of confrontation warred with my need to protect my new wife. Protecting my wife won out—easily. I wasn't going to just stand by and get high from secondhand marijuana smoke or see how it affected my wife either. As far as I was concerned, the situation was intolerable. So I marched myself down the stairs and began banging on the door to the downstairs apartment.

He didn't answer, but I could hear him moving around inside, so I yelled, "You need to stop smoking that stuff! We can smell it upstairs!" No reply. I pounded on the door again. "If you don't stop it, I'm calling the police!" No reply.

That decided it. I went back upstairs and called the police. I was in a peculiar situation. Our home was being invaded, but I didn't want to just leave. I wanted the man to stop smoking. I explained things to the police, and they promised to send a unit to investigate.

Perhaps twenty minutes later, I spotted a patrol car pulling up in front of the house. Two officers got out and came in the small little entrance way that served as a tiny lobby to the apartments. They started banging on the door like they intended to break it down. Only one problem. They were banging on my door.

I gave my wife an incredulous look and told her to wait. I went down the stairs, unlocked and opened the door. Immediately the foremost officer started yelling at me about marijuana. I held up my hand. "I'm the one who called you," I interjected when I could. "The door you want is there." I pointed to the next door.

The officer immediately looked sheepish. "Oh. Sorry. Go on back in."

I was only too glad to. I retreated and listened as they started to pound on the correct door. I figured the man inside would not answer the door. The police couldn't actually break down the door without a warrant or perhaps without more probable cause than the smell of marijuana. What I hoped would happen was that the man would stop smoking marijuana, and if he insisted on continuing, I hoped he would do it somewhere else.

Part of my plan worked. With the police on site, he did stop smoking, and the odor began to dissipate. Growing up, I had never really lived in a "bad" part of town. I had no real experience with it, and I certainly didn't know the lengths to which some people would go when you "nark" on them. I found out the next morning when I left to go to work.

When I got to the small parking lot reserved for the residents of the small apartment complex, I noticed that my car looked different. At first, I couldn't place what might be off until I got closer. Someone, and I had a pretty good idea as to who the *someone* was, had slashed all four of my tires. Nothing else was out of place, and my car was the only victim in the lot. For a long moment I just stared at flat tires, not really knowing what to do.

I was definitely going to be late for work. I looked over at the downstairs windows and thought I saw a curtain flutter as if someone had jerked back out of sight. Suspicions confirmed, at least to me, I still did not know what to do. Calling the police hadn't worked out so well for me and had only made the situation seemingly worse. With my young wife upstairs, the last thing I wanted was to get in some sort of rage war with the downstairs neighbors.

I'd have to spend $200 on tires and lose out on income from missed work, and how many times would he be able to slash my tires—seeing as he didn't have a car for me to retaliate on. I couldn't exactly stand guard on my car every night. Leaving my wife alone in this place made me feel sick. I no longer felt it safe for her to be there without me. I'd never had to deal with a situation like this before, but I knew I couldn't put my wife at risk, and I felt she was.

I ended up breaking my lease soon after this incident, and we moved in with Liberty's parents for a few months before we left to go to Colorado in early spring of 1999 to begin pastoring Gospel Light Baptist Church.

But that is not the full story. I did get my tires replaced, and I did get to work that day after seeing my wife safely with her parents. When I showed up at United Global Nippon (UGN) where I'd worked for the last three years, some of my coworkers wondered why I was late. I told them the story of what happened, and strangely, these non-Christian, foul-mouthed, irreverent men grew angry on my behalf. Three of them actually approached me later.

One said, "Tell us where you live. We'll take care of him for you."

I stared at them in utter astonishment. They were serious— deadly serious. Again, this world was one of which I was completely ignorant. I suddenly had visions of death, dismemberment, and the entire Hammond police force crawling all over my apartment, while my wife and I were interrogated for hours on end. "What?" I asked, still unsure, but fairly sure, what they were proposing.

"Look," the spokesman said, "you're a straight arrow. We see other guys from your college work here, but you actually live all that Bible stuff. We admire that, and we don't think someone should be messing with a guy like you. Tell us where you live, and we'll take care of him. He won't bother you anymore."

For the last three years, I'd tried to be a testimony for Jesus Christ and my college. Hearing that declaration of support both warmed my heart and saddened me at the same time. I hadn't realized that my efforts had paid off so well. Each of the three men proposing to "take care of my problem" had turned me down flat anytime I'd invited them to church. One of them had even mocked me and my beliefs at one time.

In a way, I'd become the pastor of those men. They'd come asking my advice on anything from God to marriage issues. They even protected me once when a man from another part of the plant offered me a calendar in a cardboard tube. Being rather naïve, I did not consider that a calendar in a sealed tube should have been a clue that *this* particular calendar might be something other than what I thought. I accepted the "gift." One of these three men offering to help take care of my evil neighbor came up and said, "Greg, do you know what type of calendar that is?"

"No," I answered, somewhat confused. After all, he was carrying one too.

"It's a porno calendar."

I had no idea! The man had protected me, knowing that I would not want such a filthy thing. He himself had no qualms about taking one, but he went out of his way to protect my Christian testimony.

These were the men ready to beat up a perfect stranger because he had messed with me. Their intent was strangely endearing—and scary. My stand had landed me in hot water with my neighbor, but with these men, it had earned their respect. Taking a stand was totally worth it!

I laughed. "No, guys. I got this."

They looked at me in disbelief. "Yeah? What are you going to do?"

"I'm going to give him a Bible."

"What?!"

"I'm going to give him a Bible," I repeated, enjoying the looks of profound astonishment all three of them wore.

They looked at each other in dismay and shook their heads. "You're crazy," one of them offered, grinning. "Just crazy."

I shrugged. "But I do want to thank you guys for the offer. I really do appreciate it."

"No problem. Let us know if you change your mind."

Taking a stand may have cost me on one hand, but I certainly gained on the other. Despite the negativity I had to endure, taking a stand was well worth the cost.

Son, what do you stand for? Don't be like a fragment of chaff that blows in whatever direction the wind is going. Take a stand.

# CHAPTER FOUR
# Know Your Own Weaknesses

Developing one's strength is easy. Being good at something lends a man a certain amount of interest in that which he is talented or skilled. However, those areas where you are weak often get overlooked and ignored. Few like to face their own weaknesses.

A weakness of mine is an easy annoyance of those who refuse to better themselves when faced with their own weaknesses. Too often I hear comments such as, "This is just the way I am," or "I can't help the way I was born," or "Why can't you accept me for the way I am?" There are aspects of a person for which those statements are absolutely true. Your likes and dislikes, for example, are often personality driven, and a personality or temperament is often something you are born with. However, that doesn't mean you can't improve areas of character in which you are lacking. And even in personality issues, we can make changes that improve our overall character.

A man should know his own weaknesses. Knowing where you are weak means you know where you can improve, but it also means you know what traps to avoid that exploit those weaknesses. Often it is the latter rather than the former that is most valuable. A weakness, by definition, can be exploited to your detriment.

Satan can and will exploit your weaknesses for his own ends. Even if you will never be truly strong in a certain area, you can walk with God so that His strength defends you against such attacks—such as availing yourself of the armor of God mentioned in Ephesians 6.

Our nature, however, is not to fix what we don't perceive as being broken. If you don't think a weakness is really a weakness or you aren't even aware of your weaknesses, you will not see dangerous moments that can exploit you and neither will you do anything to avoid the traps those weaknesses invariably set in your life.

A real man can admit weakness. The Bible commands us to confess our faults one to another.[8] Admitting weakness is humbling and can be terrifying as we fear being looked down upon by those whom we respect. These weaknesses then, even in an attempt to hide them from others, begin to dominate our lives in ways we don't perceive. They create paranoia, suspicion, and even resentment.

## The Calling of an Introvert

Growing up, I had my mind set on what I wanted to be and what I wanted to do. I wanted to be a computer systems engineer. I loved computers. My father came from a computer background, and such a career would mean I could indulge in my introverted nature. I would work well in a cubicle somewhere where I didn't have to speak to many people.

---

[8] James 5:16.

I was a rather shy boy. Girls scared me, and my introverted nature often made me vulnerable to teasing and bullying. So as a teenager, I despised most teenagers. Not only did I not feel I ever fit in, but my introverted nature along with my inability to relate to the other teenagers made me somewhat of a mystery to my peers. Their inability to understand me led to teasing and feelings of ostracizing.

I was good at sports, but I was not good at socializing. I just never got along much with my fellow teenagers. Most of my "friends" were in their mid to late twenties. On some level, I felt I could interact with them. In general, however, I just didn't much like people. I'd rather bury myself in my bedroom and read a book. I played sports and was usually one of the more talented kids on the team, but outside of that environment, I was completely out of my element when it came to interacting with others.

So when I felt God's tug on my heart to serve Him, I resisted. I felt nothing specific about the call. I just felt like most teenagers who grow up in a Bible believing, God-fearing church that there was something more to life than my own ambitions. My understanding of serving God at such a young age was fairly immature to say the least. I assumed this meant God wanted me to pastor a church or go into full-time Christian ministry in some capacity—all of which involved people. And I had problems with people.

I remember saying, "God, a pastor has to like people, and I don't. Calling me would be a mistake." Having successfully laid out my argument to God, I tried to make an end of it.

When the tour group of a Bible college came through our church, I was prepared to resist any attempt they made to recruit me. In fact, one of the girls in the group tried. Maybe they thought pretty girls would be more successful in recruiting obstinate young men, but I showed them. I defeated every attempt she made even to get me to fill out a preliminary application.

She flashed me a smile, while holding up an information card she wanted me to fill out. "It can't hurt, Greg, to fill out the card."

I folded my arms as I didn't trust them in any other position and plus it hid my hands so she couldn't thrust into my grip the pen she was trying to offer me. "I already know what I want to do. I'm going into computers."

"That's nice," she said, dismissing my chosen profession out of hand. "But there is no greater joy than to serve God."

"It's not like I'm going to abandon church," I countered. "Besides, if everyone became a pastor, who would sit in the pews?" She stared at me a bit unsure, and I congratulated myself on what I thought was profound logic. Having her on the ropes, I pressed my advantage. "Don't churches need people to teach Sunday school, or to clean the buildings, or to drive the buses? Don't churches need the tithes and offerings of the people? Doesn't it make sense that God would ask some people just to work and help support the church financially?"

She seemed to emotionally recoil with each statement. Finally, she gave up and walked off defeated. I had won! I felt rather pleased with myself, disappointed only in the fact that she had walked away. She was, after all, rather pretty.

But I failed to reckon on God.

About a year after that incident, while watching my pastor preach, I realized something profound. Not everyone would be a pastor as long as there were lost people in the world who needed to be reached with the Gospel. If we took every man in every church and sent them out to be pastors, we would still be able to fill the pews with new converts and still support each church with those converts. It dawned on me then that my pastor was doing something important.

It just clicked. I said to myself, "More people should do that." I gave a mental shrug, and then decided I'd do it. I didn't go forward. I didn't surrender at the altar. I didn't have a profound revelation. The sermon had nothing to do with surrendering to preach. I just casually volunteered. It is amazing what God can do in a person's heart when he isn't full of himself.

That decision, however, did not change who I was as a person. Having decided to go to Bible college and prepare for the ministry didn't make me any less introverted or uncomfortable around people. I knew my not liking people was a problem. Then another scary thought intruded into my brain. When you preach, people stare at you. Now that was a nightmare come true! I couldn't stand getting in front of people.

One time in high school I had to recite the poem *Eldorado* in front of the entire class. I had it down. I knew it. But the moment I stepped to the front and everyone turned his or her gaze on me, every line I'd memorized got all jumbled up into a morass of utter nonsense in my brain. I stuttered, started, stopped, and then finally looked at the teacher and in a clear voice said, "Just give me an F," and sat down.

What to do? I determined not to let this weakness conquer me. I'd probably have this weakness my entire life, but it didn't mean that I had to accept it as my fate. With God nothing is impossible.[9] So after some time in prayer, I determined to do something that was completely out of character for me. The college I attended had long hallways. Many of my peers were of the outgoing nature, and they would invariably greet me from

---

[9] Luke 1:37.

some distance before we crossed paths. I determined to greet them before they greeted me. This meant in some cases I had to shout down the hallway to someone before he could greet me.

For me to shout, "Hi, Chris!", while Chris was still fifty feet down the hall and ten people between him and me was embarrassing, but I did it. I did it until it was no longer an issue to me. I am still, by nature, an introvert. But I can crawl out of my shell and socialize—and enjoy it. I've learned not only to love people, but to like them too.

Recognizing my weakness and then knowing the pitfalls of having such a weakness led me to action that would prevent that weakness from being exploited by Satan. I went on to pastor a church for thirteen years and loved it. I loved the people—still do. God has since led me on to other avenues, but I am no longer a captive of my own weakness. Instead of it controlling me, I control it.

The freedom and opportunities that have come my way have been absolutely worth the trouble of dealing with and recognizing my weaknesses.

## The Cussing Jar

Another weakness that may have to do with my introvertish nature is that I don't do well with negative confrontations. I dread them, and this weakness then becomes a fear. But fear is a different subject; what I want to point out is how this weakness of mine dominated every aspect of my life in subtle ways that were hard to recognize.

There are times we need to confront people for their sake and for ours. Paul confronted Peter when Peter had done wrong.[10] Jesus often confronted the Pharisees, the Scribes, and the Sadducees of His day, and even drove the moneychangers out of the temple with a whip![11] Confrontation is a part of life, but I struggle mightily with it. Honest, truthful, loving, and direct confrontation is often the simplest and easiest way to resolve problems and issues. But even the possibility of having such an encounter creates a fear in me that seeks alternatives instead.

While in Bible college, I worked at United Global Nippon (UGN). We manufactured car parts that reduced sound emissions from the engine for a quieter ride. Anyone who has ever worked in a factory knows that the employees there are not the cleanest-mouthed people on the planet. Generally, they cuss up a storm. UGN was no different.

Here I was, a Bible college student training to be a pastor of a church, who had only ever spoken one cuss word out loud—in the eighth grade—having to hear constant and prolific cussing for nearly eight hours a day, five days a week. The atmosphere took its toll on me. I hated it, finding such words an irritant to my spirit. I didn't hold it against my coworkers, figuring for the most part that cussing was just the way in which they were reared. Still, I needed to do something about the language I was constantly hearing.

In most cases, a simple, honest, and straightforward confrontation done the right way would have resolved this matter for me. For the most part, my coworkers were decent men who would have tried to mitigate their language around me. But the

---

[10] Galatians 2:11.
[11] John 2:14-17.

thought of confrontation and even the vague possibility that one such confrontation might turn sour, led me to try a different approach.

I brought a very large jar to work one day and asked the shift supervisor if I could address everyone. He agreed.

"I need your help," I began. "I'm in charge of a Bible club that works with teenagers each weekend. I'd like to raise some money to help these kids, so I'd like to introduce you to my cussing jar. If you all agree, I'd like you to donate a dime for every cuss word you speak while working here. The money will go to the teenagers to help them and their families."

To be brutally honest, I didn't need the money for my Bible club. I just wanted to reduce the cussing around me, and this is how I thought of doing it. My weakness caused me to approach the situation in such a way where I perpetuated a mild deception— I actually did use the money for the teenagers, but we just didn't need it—upon the entire shift.

They loved the idea, however, and my cussing jar began to fill up. You may be asking why I didn't ask for a quarter, but honestly, they cussed so much that I didn't think they could afford a quarter for each instance. They had fun with it too. They'd catch each other cussing and make the perpetrator pay the dime. One man would walk in at the beginning of each day and stuff two or three dollars into the jar, look at me, and say, "That's for the rest of the day."

The payments did significantly reduce the cussing, and I achieved this goal in a bit of a unique manner, but I only did it that way because of my weakness. Weaknesses in our character and lives have an effect on us in subtle ways that we don't think about or anticipate. They change the way you think, the way you act, and the way you interact with others.

This story is fairly benign, but there have been other times when my weakness has only added to my problems. But by knowing my weaknesses and failings, I can work on them. I may never be strong in these areas, but I don't have to bow to them. I don't have to allow these weaknesses to dominate my life.

A man knows where he is weak and has enough character not to allow those weaknesses to stop him from doing right.

Son, what are your weaknesses? What are your limits? This doesn't mean you can't improve or get better, just as I did, but that won't happen unless you first admit you need to get better in a certain area. Where are you weak?

# CHAPTER FIVE

# Taking Responsibility for Your Actions

Manhood and growing into manhood will not be without its mistakes and deliberate wrongdoings. More manly than taking a hit in football and more courageous even than standing up for what you believe in is taking responsibility when you do wrong.

It is the rare person who doesn't offer excuses as to why he messed up, failed, or did wrong. We are born masters of finding excuses to justify failure and wrong. If there is one thing I wish every boy and man would get, it would be this: *maturity is taking responsibility for your responsibilities.* When you fail to clean your room, or fail to meet a curfew, or break something that is not yours, or show up late, or disregard a workplace rule, your ability to take responsibility for your own failures will show to what degree of maturity you possess.

When you compare King Saul to King David, you will find more similarities than differences. Both became powerful warriors and leaders. Both had humble beginnings. Both were kings of Israel. Both were chosen by God. Both were mentored by Samuel.

Both fought the Lord's battles. Both had dedicated and loyal followers. Both disobeyed the Lord's commands at least twice. Both ended up committing murder to further their own ends. So what was the difference? What distinguished David from Saul? Why did God reject Saul and call David a man after His own heart?[12]

The difference was in how David took responsibility for his sins and Saul did not. When Saul sinned, he made excuses for his actions. The first time was when he offered a sacrifice to the Lord when only the priest should have done so. Samuel was late, and a battle was eminent. Saul felt like he didn't want to go into battle without first giving an offering to God, but since Samuel was late, he made the offering in violation of God's Word.

When confronted by Samuel on this wrong, Saul gave this excuse: "Therefore said I, The Philistines will come down now upon me to Gilgal, and I have not made supplication unto the LORD: I forced myself therefore, and offered a burnt offering."[13] He claimed he forced himself, that he had no choice but to violate God's command.

Later, God commanded Saul to destroy the backstabbing, traitorous, and child-murdering Amalekites. God wanted everyone and everything destroyed, but Saul disobeyed and kept many of the best things of the Amalekites. When confronted by Samuel, he offered another excuse: "But the people took of the spoil, sheep and oxen, the chief of the things which should have been utterly destroyed, to sacrifice unto the LORD thy God in

---

[12] 1 Samuel 13:14; Acts 13:22.
[13] 1 Samuel 13:12.

Gilgal."[14] He blamed his disobedience on the people while subtly trying to justify that there was a good reason for his rebellion.

Samuel chastised Saul and pronounced, "Because thou hast rejected the word of the LORD, he hath also rejected thee from being king."[15]

This edict terrified Saul, so he sought to mitigate the disaster. Notice what he said: "I have sinned: for I have transgressed the commandment of the LORD, and thy words: because I feared the people, and obeyed their voice."[16] Even while admitting he had transgressed, he tried to excuse it by saying that he "feared the people." What? He's king! No disloyalty among the people had been reported at this time, so what in the world was he talking about? He was excusing his sin.

Saul's reaction was a far cry from David when David was caught in his sin. David's adultery and murder came to light when the prophet Nathan pointed his long bony finger at David and said, "Thou art the man!"[17]

David, instead of trying to excuse himself or justify his wrong or blame it on others, replied, "I have sinned against the LORD."[18] That was it. He was fully prepared to accept whatever punishment God would pronounce, and I personally believe he fully expected God to kill him. David even wrote a psalm about his repentance called the fifty-first Psalm. In it, he bemoans his evil and sin. There is no excuse. He puts it all on himself.

---

[14] 1 Samuel 15:21.
[15] 1 Samuel 15:23.
[16] 1 Samuel 15:24.
[17] 2 Samuel 12:7.
[18] 2 Samuel 12:13.

At another point, David numbers the people. Numbering the people was the preliminary step to going to war. Jesus obliquely refers to this numbering in Luke when He said, "Or what king, going to make war against another king, sitteth not down first, and consulteth whether he be able with ten thousand to meet him that cometh against him with twenty thousand?"[19] Joab, David's general, went out to number the warriors, but God had not commanded David to go to war. Worse, David was relying on strength of numbers to carry the victory instead of God's power. This insult and lack of faith was in direct violation of God's Word.

Once again, confronted with his sin, David made no excuse: "I have sinned greatly, because I have done this thing: but now, I beseech thee, do away the iniquity of thy servant; for I have done very foolishly."[20]

David was used mightily by God. Saul was set aside. The only real difference recorded in their lives was the way they handled their own wrongdoings. Saul made excuses; David did not. One showed cowardliness. The other showed manliness.

## Benefiting from Wrongdoing

I grew up playing soccer, and despite my skinny frame, I was good at the sport. We won more games than we lost, I was the top scorer, and I loved it. Soccer, like any sport, has rules to keep the game from breaking down into chaos and an utter free-for-all. These rules have penalties when broken, which mean the rules have value.

---

[19] Luke 14:31.
[20] 1 Chronicles 21:8.

Breaking the rules is a no-no, but like most people, I was fully willing to break a rule if I saw that an advantage could be gained by doing so. This might be a cultural thing in the United States, but I suspect it is more of a sin-nature thing that we are all born with. Pushing boundaries and bending or breaking rules to gain an advantage is not something we teach children. It is something we are born with.

In one particular game of soccer when I was maybe in the fifth or sixth grade, I chose to break a rule because the advantage of breaking the rule outweighed the advantage the other team had if I did not. In basketball parlance, we call this a "good foul"—a "good bad," in other words. If that phrase is not an oxymoron, then I don't know what is!

A kid on the other team got on a breakaway and streaked toward our goal with the ball. I was in a position to catch him, so I shot off after him. I quickly saw that I didn't have a chance to cut him off, and the goalie on my team was flat-footed, standing on the goal line instead of running out in an attempt to cut off the angle of shots the opposing player had.

I realized the kid would be able to take the ball practically to the goal line before making a shot into that huge, wide-open net. I was right behind him when we entered the penalty box, and I made a calculated decision. If I did nothing, the kid would score easily. If I interfered, and broke the rules, then even if I got called for it, the kid would have to make a penalty shot from distance instead of the can't-miss-for-anything shot my goalie was offering to him.

So I pushed him. Not hard, mind you, just enough to cause him to stumble and accidently kick the ball right into the waiting arms of my goalie. Everyone knew I had pushed him—except one. The kids, parents, and coaches of the other team were hopping-angry, yelling and pointing. My team, my coach, and every parent on my side of the field stood in dead silence, waiting for the call that would give the other team a penalty kick.

But it never came.

The referee had been immediately behind the two of us as we streaked down the soccer pitch. He couldn't see the push. From his perspective, the other kid just stumbled and muffed the shot. So he didn't do anything, and play continued.

I didn't know the referee couldn't see what I'd done. I fully expected to be penalized, but I figured the advantage my team would gain for breaking the rules would be much better than the advantage the kid on the other team had gained by his speed and skill. Being young and having the implicit approval of my coach and team for my clever actions, I said nothing, and even felt a sense of elation that I'd gotten away with breaking the rules. It was a "good foul"—a "good bad."

Despite the other team's attempt to force me to be penalized for my wrongdoing, I got away with it. I didn't have to take responsibility for my actions. And even if I'd been caught, I wouldn't have minded, figuring the penalty kick would be better for us than letting the kid just dribble the ball into the goal.

This is an interesting case where the wrongdoing had benefits no matter what the consequences were to me or my team—except one.

I learned the wrong lesson.

I learned that there were times when breaking a rule was good. I could do a "good wrong." But in life, there should be no such thing. Life isn't so black and white that we can easily distinguish what the right thing always is. As already mentioned, you would lie to save someone's life. You'd do a "good wrong."

This gray area of morality exists because of sin. It creates an environment wherein even taking responsibility for our actions can result in a deliberate and willful act of wrongdoing. This won't go away this side of heaven, but every young man must be aware of this gray area of life, seek to mitigate his actions, be willing to take responsibility for his wrongs, to be forthcoming with his wrongdoings, and take whatever the consequences are.

Other than not pushing the player on the other team, I should've also admitted my wrong. No one on my team would have wanted me to do that. Everyone wanted me to keep my mouth shut, and with having their implicit approval to do so, that is what I did. But even that was wrong. I didn't take responsibility for my actions. I got away with wrongdoing and was much more likely to do it again now that I'd gotten away with it.

That is the real danger. Once you start down a road of successfully breaking the rules and getting away with it, the odds of your doing it again are much greater—and doing so even when the advantages of doing the right thing far outweigh any advantage gained by doing wrong. Because of what I had done, I would be more apt to push a player when a shot on goal wasn't on the line, when he was just in my way, when I just was too lazy to run a player down and take the ball. I would think of other opportunities where a push could be used to my immediate advantage. This is a natural and hidden consequence of even doing a "good wrong."

Real men look for ways to do right—not ways to do wrong. And when they do wrong, they stand up and take the consequences like men.

# Taking Responsibility for Another's Impression

Perhaps one of the most valuable lessons I ever learned came from my parents one day when I had to take a chewing out for something I didn't do.

A guest speaker came to our church to conduct a revival when I was ten or eleven. At the time, our church met in a small storefront in Mesa, Arizona. I sat next to my mom and brother during the service. A couple of kids behind us started to act up during the preaching, and the evangelist happened to catch them out of the corner of his eyes. When he whipped around, he ended up focusing on me as I also turned around to see what was happening.

The other kids, with their instinctual ability to know when to stop goofing off when attention from someone in authority was turned on them, were suddenly little angels, sitting still and pretty as if they'd never moved an inch the entire service.

So the only movement the evangelist could clearly see was me. The evangelist focused on me and said, "Son, you don't act that way in church. You need to sit still and be quiet!" He said that, of course, using his microphone so the entire church heard it, and, of course, every eye turned to look at me.

I wanted to get up and protest. I really wanted my parents to get up and protest, but my mom laid a hand on my arm to keep me still. For the rest of the sermon, I fumed in my seat. The injustice of it all! I hadn't done a single thing wrong, and I was the one called down for it.

I didn't hear the rest of the sermon. I was just waiting for it to end because I knew that once it was over, my mom would go and straighten out the evangelist's mistake. I looked forward to him apologizing to me, and it would be sweet revenge if he would apologize to me in front of the whole congregation. After all, he had humiliated me in front of everyone, so why shouldn't he be humiliated in turn?

Things didn't go the way I hoped—not by a long shot.

As soon as the service ended, my mother leaned over, looked at me, and said, "Son, go and apologize to the preacher."

I sat in stunned silence. When I found my voice, I protested, "But Mom! I didn't do anything wrong! It was those other kids!"

She nodded. "I know. But that isn't the point. The preacher thinks it was you. You shouldn't want his last impression of you to be one of misbehaving." She paused, looking me over as if trying to take my measure. "You could try to straighten him out, Son, but will he believe you?"

"You could tell him," I pointed out.

She shook her head. "I could, but it won't accomplish the one thing that I want—that you should want. He won't see you, Son, the real you. He will only see that he was corrected. He might apologize to you—to us, but will that change what happened? Will he think of you any differently? You would become the source of his embarrassment. Is that what you want?"

Truthfully, in a way it was, but then in a way it wasn't either. I didn't want the evangelist to think of me as a troublemaker. I indicated the real troublemakers who were scrambling toward the church exit. "They should be the ones to apologize," I mumbled, still trying to find a way out.

"That's their problem," Mom said. "That's on them, and they'll have to live with themselves."

"It's not fair."

My mother smiled. "You're right. It isn't. Sometimes you have to take responsibility for what other people think about you, even if they are mistaken. Who else is going to change the way they think? By apologizing, you make him see you—the real you."

I couldn't believe it. I cast about for some other way out of the mess and found none. I nodded, swallowed my young pride, and made my way up to the front where the evangelist was standing talking to those who came to thank him for his sermon.

I waited until the last person had finished shaking his hand and then stepped up to him—though I didn't offer my hand. "I'm sorry for misbehaving," I said.

He took a long look at me, considering. Finally, he bent over and put his hands on my shoulders. "I really appreciate that, son. What's your name?"

"Greg."

"Well, Greg, it takes a real man to do what you just did." He smiled. "I'm impressed."

I returned his smile, feeling much better. I never got the opportunity to straighten out the preacher's mistake, but I did get him to see me in a different light. By taking responsibility for the way he thought of me, I was able to accomplish something I never would have been able to do otherwise.

Misunderstandings are a natural part of life. If you don't take responsibilities for the misunderstandings you helped create accidently or otherwise, you may not get people to see the real you. Misunderstandings create impressions, and impressions linger unless they are dealt with in the right way. So taking responsibility helps create new impressions.

Son, what sort of man have you become in this area? Do you try to get out of trouble or do you take responsibility for what you've done?

# CHAPTER SIX
# Courage and Fear

A man should be courageous. Being courageous does not mean he has no fear. In fact, *courage* is at its core the ability to overcome one's fear. So a courageous man does not allow fear to dominate or rule his life. Instead, he learns to control and dominate his fear. The Bible teaches that God has not given us the spirit of fear.[21] That verse does not mean that a spirit of fear doesn't exist. Satan can introduce such a spirit into our lives, but generally speaking, our own insecurities and weaknesses will create this spirit of fear just as easily.

With that said, fear is not necessarily bad or that all fear is wrong. A healthy fear can keep you from making mistakes, making bad decisions, or doing something foolish. The right fear can be a powerful motivator. The Bible teaches that Noah built the ark because he was moved with fear.[22] He feared that if he did not obey God, he and his family would die. He knew what was coming, and his fear drove him to build the ark.

---

[21] 2 Timothy 1:7.
[22] Hebrews 11:7.

As a young teenager, I sometimes took a recurve bow, jumped the fence of my backyard into the softball fields belonging to the adjacent junior high school, and shot arrows. Only I shot these arrows straight up with the goal of seeing how close I could get them to fall next to me. I found there was a trick to it. As long as you could see the arrow in the air, it would not land near you, but if you lost sight of it, then you would be looking at only the tiny, invisible tip. When that happened, it was time to run!

During one such exhibition of pure foolishness, I shot an arrow straight up, lost sight of it, and so wisely ran away. I took no more than three steps when I realized one of my cats had followed me out into the field, and when I started running, it started running too, directly to the spot where I anticipated the arrow to land.

With my heart in my throat—I liked that particular cat—I spun and ran at Shadow, yelling to scare him away. He ran, but that arrow came down right behind me and landed no more than six feet away. The fear that came with that close call gave me a bit of additional wisdom, and I stopped shooting arrows straight up. So you see, sometimes fear can keep you from doing something foolish.

In fact, there is another type of "good" fear. God commands us to serve Him with reverence and godly fear.[23] Specifically, we are warned that God is a consuming fire,[24] and for that reason, we should serve Him with a godly fear instead of some flippant, half-hearted, lackadaisical attitude. With that said, a man should never let fear control his life. Insecurities lead to fears. Fears lead to panic

---

[23] Hebrews 12:28.
[24] Hebrews 12:29.

or hasty decisions that are later regretted. Giving into fear is also habit forming. Fear can turn into a phobia if not addressed. Perhaps the worst fear is the fear of the unknown.

## The Pseudo Mountain Lion

I didn't do it often, but I did go hunting on occasion while growing up. On one particular hunt as a 14-year-old, I positioned myself along the top of a ridge with a fairly open view below where I thought a game trail crossed. I intended to sit in ambush and wait for some clueless buck to cross paths in the crosshairs of my .243 Winchester.

I sat waiting for perhaps an hour when an odd, totally unfamiliar sound coming from the bottom of the hill began to drift up to my ears. It sounded like something walking, but in a rhythm that didn't fit any gait I could picture.

Whatever it was, it moved slowly up the hillside in my general direction with infuriating sluggishness. Then I spotted something moving low in a stunted pine tree about three quarters of the way down the hill. I knew the animal couldn't be a deer; the proportions were all wrong. I raised up my scope and centered the crosshairs on the spot. What I saw gave me a hasty pause, for what I saw looked exactly like the hood a hunter might wear.

My heart thumped as I realized I might be pointing my rifle at another human being, and knowing what my dad would do to me if he found out, I hastily lowered my rife. Whatever was down there had no intention of being quiet, however. It moved, making those strange sounds that I just couldn't place.

At first, I felt irritated. *This is my hill. I was here first!* Since the hunter below me had taken a spot that meant he was pretty much in front of me no matter where I shot, I would either have to move or he would. Being only fourteen, I didn't relish asking the other hunter to move. So I thought I'd better move, but something kept me from getting up, and I continued to watch.

After a time, I determined it had to be an animal. No *human would act like that.* So risking my father's wrath, I raised my rife and sighted through the scope to see if I could determine what kind of animal I was dealing with. Deep shadows from the pine tree obscured much of what I could see. I waited, holding my breath. When the unknown animal moved again, my heart stopped.

I saw what I was sure was the snout of a mountain lion. I began shaking. I didn't much care about being in the woods with a hungry mountain lion. The scope of my rifle began shaking all over the place, looking like I was caught in a massive earthquake. I felt like it too. I took the safety off and tried to steady the rifle by bracing my arm against one knee.

I tried to recall anything I could about mountain lions, but nothing came to mind. I gripped the rifle tightly and stilled it as best I could, then placed my finger on the trigger. I didn't pull it, however. I was still too shaky, and my scope wouldn't cooperate and stay centered enough for me to shoot.

The lion moved, dipping down and temporarily out of my sights. I pulled back and waited. The last thing I wanted was to be stalked by a mountain lion in the forested mountains of Arizona somewhere south of Flagstaff. I licked my lips and thought about yelling for my dad, but my father had gone off in another direction sometime ago, and I had no idea if he was even within earshot. I felt hot, the cool mountain air unable to compete with the heat my fear generated.

Then I saw the animal making its way up the hill directly toward me. But what I saw was no mountain lion charging my position. It wasn't even a human. A slow-moving porcupine continued to amble slowly up the hill. My fear bled away like so much water from a leaky canteen.

Now that I knew for a fact what the object of my fear was, I became curious. I clamored to my feet as the animal approached me. The porcupine neither seemed surprised or terribly interested in the lanky youth who carried an odd-shaped stick. It continued to plod along at a sedate pace right past me, comfortable in its armor.

I never did see any deer, but the porcupine I will never forget. The fear of the unknown loomed large in my mind. Years later, as an adult, I wrote a short story based on this experience to illustrate how we can so easily let our fears create imaginary monsters that simply don't exist and how fear can dominate our thinking and actions.

I share that short story below.

## Alone in the Valley of Shadow – A Short Story

I love to hike in the mountains. And, if I may boast, I never get lost. Usually. This time, when the clouds rolled in, obscuring the sun and casting everything into deep shadows, I knew I was in trouble. Suddenly everything began to blend together. Colors faded from the landscape, and the ominous clouds hid any hint of the sun's location. I halted my return trek and looked around nervously.

I stood in a shallow valley nestled between three peaks of equal height and proportions. Pine trees and shadow obscured much of what could be seen in dark shades of green. In front of me, the valley split around one of the peaks, confusing me. I didn't remember from which direction I had come. I wasn't even sure I had been here before. I began chewing on my lower lip, uncertain. You might be wondering where my compass was, and by this time so was I. I hadn't thought to bring it—after all, I *never* got lost.

Until now, that is.

I held my breath to listen better and heard a faint rushing sound, but the sound could have been the breeze rustling through the treetops or the hollowness of the silence enveloping me. I kicked a loose stone just to prove my hearing hadn't deserted me all together. For some reason, I felt reluctant to say anything, as if speaking aloud would only serve to emphasize how utterly alone I was.

For the first time, I really began to understand what it was like to be alone. Sometimes, we seek to be alone to gain some measure of peace from a frantic world, to flee some of the pressures of life, or to escape a turbulent relationship. But even in such loneliness, there is the knowledge that you can return to the lives of others. There is the comfort of being able to find your way back to the company of others and that others can find you.

Where I stood, however, I felt completely cut off. I didn't know how to get back, and I doubted anyone would stumble across me way out here. This is true loneliness—a feeling I cared not to repeat.

I studied the clouds, the peaks, and the forest for some sign of civilization, anything that would give me a direction. And that's when I heard it. A faint sound like pebbles being dropped onto larger stones. The noise then stopped abruptly after a few seconds. My eyes narrowed, and I cocked my head to listen better. Had I imagined it?

No. I could hear it again, drawing closer. It stopped once more. I couldn't pinpoint the direction the noise had come from.

My heart began to pound, for I knew that nothing natural made that sound. *Something* was coming. Hoping the noise was human in origin, I cleared my throat and called, "Hello? Anyone there?" My voice sounded foreign even to my own ears.

No one responded, but a cascade of pebbles caught my attention, and I swung in that direction trying to spot the cause. I saw a shadow disappear into the deeper shadows of the trees somewhat higher on one of the slopes.

*Something is stalking me!*

My imagination went wild. I thought of everything from a mountain lion to a grizzly bear. I backed off a few paces, my heart sounding overly loud to my ears. I stared hard at the spot where the shadow had slipped from my view.

If I had felt alone before, the feeling just intensified a thousand-fold. I began a silent prayer then, calling upon the only person I believed could possibly come to my aid: God. Not being a very religious man, I felt somewhat awkward doing so. I licked my lips, apologized to God for everything I could think of, and silently begged, "Get me out of here, please!"

The sound came again, and something moved deep within the shadows. *Okay, enough of this.* I bolted down the mountainside.

Trees flashed by, and I flinched violently whenever my clothing got snagged on a branch. I dodged where I could, ducked when I had to, and jumped the larger rocks that impeded my flight. On one such jump, I landed all wrong, twisted my ankle, and fell hard. Pain fired up my leg, and I yelped as I rolled over and over. I finally came to a painful stop next to a twisted tree, trying to grow between two giant boulders.

I lay there for a long time, trying to catch my breath and control the pain. When at last I worked my way into a sitting position, I found myself facing the direction from which I had come. For all of my panicked flight, I had perhaps gained no more than fifty yards of distance from my starting point. Not very far at all.

Again, I cried out to God for help. My situation, if anything, had just gotten worse. I was not only lost, alone, and being stalked by some unknown animal, I was now hurt and injured.

The sound I now feared the most reached my ears, and I froze, listening hard. I recognized the sound for what it really was—claws clicking on rocks. This was no deer or other animal that would likely flee a human presence! No, this animal was deliberately coming right at me. It didn't hurry, but came on in a measured stalking pace, seemingly in no rush to finish me off.

I felt a wetness trickle down the side of my face and realized I had cut my scalp in my headlong roll. Most likely, whatever predator was approaching could now smell blood—my blood!

I was terrified. Keeping my eyes on the vegetation in front of me, I felt around until my hand found a decent-sized stone. At least I would have something to throw. I sat very still, praying the animal would not see me, would just move around me, and would just leave me alone!

And then I saw it.

Not clearly, mind you, but I saw it move up into the low branches of a pine tree, shadow against shadow. With the clouds obscuring the sun, and the gray light fast fading, I couldn't clearly distinguish what it was. It merely sat there, within the shadow of the tree, staring at me and making a gnawing noise that sent shivers down my spine.

I swallowed hard and felt its beady eyes upon me. My nemesis not only knew where I was, it knew of my helpless state. It just watched from within the shadow of the tree, continuing to make that dreadful gnawing sound—taunting me. I was dead. I just knew it.

In desperation, I threw my rock at it. It fell short, of course. I lacked the strength to hurl it properly. The creature took no notice other than to pause in its gnawing to regard me menacingly.

And then my adversary waddled out from underneath the tree and came toward me.

Yes, waddled, for the dreadful creature stalking me was a porcupine. A porcupine! It moved toward me or rather toward another pine tree to begin gnawing on the bark, eating away while regarding me with a bored eye. The animal did indeed know me, and he held no fear of me. His protective quills were all the deterrent he needed to keep me at bay.

I breathed a huge sigh of relief and relaxed against my own tree. Only then did I realize what I had done. My fear had now created a worse scenario than the one in which I had originally found myself. I had a badly sprained ankle, as well as bruises and cuts all over from my fall. And I was still lost and alone. A childhood Bible verse floated to my mind, though I suspect God had something to do with the thought: "Yea, though I walk through the valley of the shadow of death, I will fear no evil: for thou art with me; thy rod and thy staff they comfort me."

I recognized that the man in the verse hadn't entered the valley of shadow without first knowing God would be at his side. He had gone in prepared. If I had started my trek through the mountains a bit more prepared, perhaps with a compass and a sidearm, I would not have feared the approaching porcupine. My own overconfidence and lack of foresight were my undoing.

The porcupine waddled on by, keeping a wary eye trained on me. I paid the animal no heed. I sat wondering what I was to do. I was a long way from help, and the gray light was fast slipping away into night. I wanted to yell at God and blame Him, but I realized I probably should have involved God before my troubles began— before I ever came to this valley of shadow.

Suddenly another sound, from a different direction than the porcupine had taken, reached my ears. I swallowed hard, and fear began to creep back into the recesses of my mind. I licked my lips and yelled, "Hello? Anyone there?" My voice broke, and I felt the sting of sweat mingling with the blood on my forehead.

No answer. Just the sounds of something approaching. The shadows in the valley deepened, verging on darkness. Now, I only had my fear to keep me company...and whatever approached. Oh, how I wished I'd have begun this journey better prepared!

Once again, I began to pray.

## Facing My Fears

I do have a minor fear of heights. I'm not terrified of heights, but I certainly don't want to get too close to the edge of a long drop off. We all have fears that haunt us and fears that manipulate our decisions and thoughts. While my fear of heights does not detract from my life much, I have another fear that does.

I fear confrontations, particularly one-on-one negative confrontations.

This real fear of mine has followed me since childhood. I just don't do well with negative confrontations. I start to shake, my mouth turns dry, and my ability to think clearly decreases. I can do it, but getting into an argument where personalities are involved is something I simply do not handle well. Arguing with people about differences of opinions doesn't bother me as long as our personalities don't clash and we start attacking each other. But the moment someone attacks me as a person or I have to correct someone or face someone as an opponent, my fear comes to the front full force.

Often, I bulldoze my way through it, but to say that my fear doesn't affect my thinking and even my decision making would be erroneous. When faced with a confrontation, I may try to put it off or simply mitigate the necessity of the confrontation as an excuse not to deal with the situation directly. My fear is tied to my introverted nature, I know, so in order to deal with it effectively, I have to face these fears.

When in the fifth grade, I attended Eastside Christian School. During recess, a bunch of us boys would go outside to play soccer. There was no problem with that, but several of the older seventh and eighth grade boys would love to intercept the soccer ball and kick it as far away from the soccer field as they could and laugh while one of us younger boys ran after it.

Despite my fear of confrontation, I eventually grew tired of this day-in, day-out intrusion into our game. So I positioned myself to interfere with the next eighth grader who wanted to disrupt our soccer game. My opportunity came quickly. An eighth grader darted out from his group of fellow bullies and ran after a loose soccer ball to kick it far and long. Having played soccer for many years, I simply intercepted and slide-tackled him—properly, mind you. I slid into the ball so that when he went to kick it, the ball didn't go anywhere, but he did. He flew over the ball and landed roughly in the grass and dirt, getting a nice scrape on one elbow.

What happened next was not part of what I'd planned. For some strange reason, he took exception to being tripped up by a skinny fifth grader, so he came at me swinging. I'd never been in a fight before. I'd never punched someone or been punched by someone who really meant to do me bodily harm. I backpedaled, but he kept coming. I reacted instinctively, ducked under his punch, and used his momentum to jerk him to the ground where I proceeded to sit on him until a teacher could come over and rescue me.

Not being very big or heavy, keeping his back turned toward me was a chore, but being wiry allowed me to keep him off balance and unable to land any real punches. When the teacher came over and pulled me off him, I was shaking like a leaf. My mouth felt as if I hadn't had any water in years. I shook for at least the next half hour. I was probably feeling something similar to what some soldiers feel after battle or others after serious injury. It was a form of shock, but as a direct result of my fear, not of actually being injured.

I played on the chess team of Gilbert High School for two and a half years. Chess is played against a single opponent, and anytime I played someone I didn't know, I would begin to shake, and my mouth would turn dry. Playing a chess match was a type of one-on-one confrontation, and I didn't like such confrontations. One-on-one confrontations were the source of my fear. I would have this feeling for a good part of the game before I could settle down and simply play. My fear interfered with my ability to think clearly, and I often lost because of a stupid or hasty move.

Halfway through my junior year in high school, I quit playing and used the excuse that it was interfering with my academics. In truth, playing three games of chess in a tournament where each game could last nearly two and a half hours took its toll on me emotionally and mentally. Each game was a struggle, for each game meant I had to confront a stranger over a chessboard. Each game meant my hands would turn shaky, my mouth would go dry, and my heart would begin to beat faster. I felt so drained, so emotionally wiped out that I finally told my chess coach I had to quit.

I had let my fear control me, so I took the path of least resistance so that I wouldn't have to face my fears. Failing to face my fear hurt me, and I missed out on some interesting opportunities. Once I graduated from high school, I resolved to no longer let my fears control me.

I have come to learn that this fear is not going away. It is part of my nature. So I choose not to let it control me. I purposely allow myself to be put into positions where I must face this fear. I don't try to avoid it anymore. I pastored a church for thirteen years and had many confrontations. These incidents took their toll on me, and they always will, but I cannot hide from life. I can't avoid people, and I can't avoid one-on-one confrontations. So I don't worry about it anymore. I gave it to God, and when I am faced with such a confrontation, I still shake, my mouth still gets dry, my heart still thumps, and my mind still doesn't work as clearly as I'd like—but I no longer use my fear as an excuse.

I choose not to live in fear. I might make a great hermit, but people are important. And since people are often the source of my phobia, I deliberately interact with people. Your own fears will dominate your thinking and your decision making, but that is no excuse to hide from your fears. Fears must be faced to be overcome. I faced my fears, and I am so glad I did. I cannot imagine living in a world where I only sought to avoid what I most feared. How many friends would I have lost over the years? How many blessings would I have missed out on? How many opportunities would have passed me by?

Being a man doesn't mean you don't have fears, but being a man means you should be willing to face your fears. A man never lets his fears control him.

Son, what do you fear the most? What fear is controlling your life?

# CHAPTER SEVEN
# Liking Yourself

Son, so many young men reach a point in their teenage years where they don't like themselves all that much. This may be true for you. Perhaps you were made fun of for the way you look. Perhaps your peers called you stupid. Maybe you were the last one picked for a team. Maybe you look in the mirror and you don't like what you see. Maybe you don't feel like you fit in—that you're an outsider. Maybe you wish you were smarter, more athletic, more popular, more handsome, or possessed a quick wit.

What people say about you helps form your own opinion of who you are. When you start comparing yourself to others or have others compare you to another, the results can be discouraging. I'm not even sure it is possible *not* to do this. Realizing my own weaknesses, for example, can only happen when I recognize them as weaknesses, and to do that, comparisons must be made. The problem comes when instead of trying to improve himself, the person comes to dislike himself.

A real man is comfortable in his own skin. He improves where he can and what he can, but sometimes, he needs to learn to like himself as he is. Some boys who can't or won't like himself may retreat into a fantasy world where he is someone different, someone who fits his idea of what he would like to be. In this fantasy world, he is the hero—the most capable, the strongest, the most intelligent, and the most skilled person.

When reality disappoints, these boys will retreat into this fantasy world they've created. Unfortunately, this fantasy world begins to have priority over reality, and their reality suffers even more. Their grades could suffer in school. Their ability to relate to people and make friends suffers. They cannot take advantage of opportunities because such realities actually interfere with their fantasy world. Retreating into a fantasy world is not a healthy escape.

I didn't have many friends growing up. And once I got into high school, I struggled because I was so skinny, lacking in good looks, and unable to fit in with the other kids. I began to read an abundance of fantasy novels, and those stories helped create a world to which I could retreat—a world where I was the most powerful person. I would fantasize about great feats of arms, of daring rescues, of amazing martial arts skills, and so on. In my fantasy world where I mattered, people noticed me, and I could shine. As I grew older and I began to crave the attention of girls, I began to fantasize about girls, specifically about being their hero and rescuing them from some danger or evil. This fantasy world, however, became more beloved and desired than the reality in which I lived. I was in very real danger of sabotaging my future.

This dislike of yourself creates doubt about anything you can do. The Bible says, "Beloved, if our heart condemn us not, then have we confidence toward God."[25] If your own heart dislikes yourself, then how can you have confidence that God loves you? If you think you are worthless, then how can you trust that God

---

[25] 1 John 3:21.

thinks you are important? If you think you don't deserve to live, then how can you be confident that God has a special job for your life?

Son, the key to liking yourself is gaining confidence in some aspect of reality. This is not the same as overconfidence, but rather about gaining the needed confidence that you are who God made you to be and that you can do what God created you to do. The Bible warns us not to cast away our confidence.[26] This reference, mentioned in Hebrews, is specifically about salvation because the moment we cast away our confidence in Jesus Christ, we begin to face overwhelming doubt. Paul wrote to the Philippian people to tell them they could be confident that "he which hath begun a good work in you will perform it until the day of Jesus Christ."[27] A few verses later, Paul said, "Nevertheless to abide in the flesh is more needful for you. And having this confidence, I know that I shall abide and continue with you all for your furtherance and joy of faith."[28] Paul knew that he was needed, and this knowledge gave him confidence to continue.

You see, Paul dreamed of leaving this world and being with Christ.[29] In a way, this was his fantasy world—one he wished he could soon be part of. But because he knew he was needed on earth and he still had a purpose, he had the confidence to continue doing what God had asked of him. He could suffer any wrong and pain because he knew he was needed.

Son, you need to seek God's place for you. Everyone has a place at every stage of his life. Your place right now needs you to

---

[26] Hebrews 10:35.
[27] Philippians 1:6.
[28] Philippians 1:24-25.
[29] Philippians 1:23.

fill it, and once you've found your place in Christ, you can find the confidence you need to be comfortable in your own skin. Once you are comfortable in what and who God made you to be at this moment, then even when you are attacked, made fun of, ridiculed, or teased, you can just shrug it off—even with humor. Confidence gives you this ability.

## Chicken Legs

I was often bothered by how skinny I was. I remember in junior high school going to the gym with my class, and I couldn't even bench press a hundred pounds. Some guys in my eighth-grade class seemed to have bulging muscles and could bench two hundred pounds or more. Their strength made me feel inadequate. My face, which looked like someone had squeezed it, was thin, and in my opinion, it wasn't a very handsome face.

I hadn't filled out much by the time I got into college. My college yearbook photos show a pinched-faced, skinny kid who didn't really look old enough even to be in college. But within the first two years of college, I found my equilibrium and became comfortable in my own skin. This capability became evident to me when my skinniness was made fun of by a school nurse.

I had sprained my ankle while playing volleyball with some teenagers the day before. I was in quite a bit of pain, but all I wanted was a crutch so I could limp to church that Sunday morning. The on-duty nurse was an upperclassman college girl in charge of determining whether or not someone's illness or injury was sufficient to excuse them from church or the person needed to be admitted to the infirmary. I only needed a crutch, and I could hop along just fine.

She must have had a bad morning. I distinctly remember one guy in line ahead of me arguing adamantly with her about how ill he was and that he needed to stay in the dorms and be excused from church. He was so vigorous about the matter that I nearly told him to shut up and man up, but the nurse threw up her arms and gave in. After writing him a note that granted him his excuse, she turned to me.

"What's wrong with you?" she demanded. She was a pretty thing, I noted to myself, and she seemed well-proportioned—not at all like me.

I tried to give her my best disarming smile. I didn't want to get on her bad side. "I sprained my ankle."

She glanced at my ankle still covered by my trousers leg. "Well? Let's see it then."

I pulled up the leg of my trousers to bare my swollen ankle. With her lips pursed, she studied my ankle and my hairy leg. "You've got chicken legs," she said almost absently.

*Chicken legs!? Chicken legs! Where did that come from?* I actually thought her absentminded comment was funny, so I laughed and gestured at my skinny body. "Take a look at the rest of me. Did you really expect anything else?"

She glanced up at me, and a faint blush spread across her cheeks as she belatedly realized she might have just insulted me. "Do you want a note to stay in the dorms?" she asked to cover her embarrassment.

I shook my head. "I just need a crutch."

She looked relieved. "Thank you," she said simply. "I'm getting tired of having to treat wimpy men."

That remark made me feel good. Despite the fact that I had chicken legs in her mind, my determination not to miss church and not to use her as an excuse to stay in the dorms went a long way to raise myself in her estimation. I couldn't do anything about my skinny chicken legs, but I didn't need to. I didn't once feel offended or embarrassed. My legs were the way they were, but by doing right, I gained confidence in myself.

It's amazing how things you might be sensitive to can be overlooked when you have confidence in yourself.

## Pig One, Kid Zero

Several times while growing up, my family would go my uncle's farm in Indiana. It was a trip, let me tell you, especially if you drove. Being only eight on this particular trip, it didn't really matter to me. I didn't have to drive or pay attention to where we were or where we were going.

A farm to a city kid is both a place of wonder and apprehension. The animals all looked big and dangerous—even the chickens seemed to eye me with a particular malevolence as if just daring me to get too close. My uncle raised pigs that once they reached a certain age and weight would be slaughtered, and the meat sold. One particular pig was ripe for the slaughterhouse, and my uncle needed to get the pig into the back of his truck.

I offered to help. My uncle seemed somewhat dubious, but agreed. "When I get the pig into the truck," he explained, "you need to keep it from running back out while I jump the fence and set the gate of the truck. Do you understand?"

I thought so. I reviewed what my uncle needed me to do in my mind. *All I need to do is keep the pig from crashing back through the gate of the chute. How hard can that be?* I was bigger than that stupid pig. I mentally flexed my muscles. *No problem.*

"The chute gate won't close all the way," he continued, "so you'll have to stand there and make sure that pig doesn't escape. Don't back down." My uncle gave me a stern look. "If you stay in his way, he'll be the one that backs down. Understand?"

His explanation sounded reasonable. "I understand."

Loading the pig took time. That ornery pig must've sensed what was in store for it if it got in that truck, so it about did everything in its power to keep away from my uncle. Uncle Ralph needed nearly thirty minutes to trap that pig and shoo it up the ramp and into the truck.

The moment that pig ran into the chute, my uncle yelled, "Close the gate!"

Waiting for that signal, I pushed the gate close, while my uncle jumped the fence in an effort to set the truck gate and trap the pig. But the moment that pig found himself at a dead end in that truck bed, it spun around, snorted, took one look at the scrawny eight-year-old boy standing between it and freedom and charged.

As warned, the chute gate wouldn't close all the way, so I stood in the small gap between the gate and the fence, blocking the only means that pig had of escape. The pig loomed larger and larger at it rushed me, and suddenly I'd never seen a pig so big, so mean-looking, and with such hate-filled eyes. One look into its piggish eyes and I knew, and I mean I *knew*, that that pig meant to bowl me right over and trample me into the ground—for starters.

*No sir.* I wisely scrambled out of the way, and that pig, squealing something awful, squeezed through the narrow opening I'd left and dashed back out into the hog pen.

"Gregory!" my uncle roared, lurching up to the fence. His deeply tanned face looked red as he glared at me. "I told you to stand your ground!"

"I'm sorry," I wailed, realizing that my uncle would have to take another thirty minutes to round up that pig. "I couldn't—"

"Never mind," he snapped. "Just get out of the way. I'll do it myself." He stormed off.

I felt bad. Very bad. The image I'd created of being able do battle with that pig had crumbled. My confidence was shattered. Hurt, I scrambled out of the pen and walked away. I never offered to help my uncle again. First, I felt I would fail even if I did. Second, I didn't want to see that look of disgust in my uncle's face again. No doubt my uncle was working on a timetable, and he didn't want to have to spend another thirty minutes doing the job he'd just completed. He wasn't as much upset with me as he was with having to do the job all over again. But to my eight-year-old brain, I believed he was angry with me. One thing was for sure: I didn't want to be a farmer.

Once my confidence had been shattered, I became insecure about myself. Son, this will happen to you at some point in your life. You'll fail at something, and someone will make a big deal about your failure. You won't think you can do the job well, so you'll not want to do the job at all. Seeing yourself as a failure will cripple you in the future. You won't like yourself in moments like that, but if you keep your confidence in the Lord, you'll be able to bounce back.

# CHAPTER EIGHT
# Thank God! I'm a Failure!

The title of this chapter may sound odd, but I do hope you fail, son. This is because true success is built upon the foundation of failure. Success, which is different than accomplishment, can only happen after you've failed. Many people accomplish great things, but those accomplishments do not make them successful. People born with great talent can accomplish great things with that talent. Neither do those accomplishments mean they're successful.

Success is the overcoming of your failures. It is taking your failure and using it as a platform to succeed. Success is constant movement whereas accomplishment is a fixed point in time. Successful people are in a constant state of forward motion in life. Accomplishment is never something you're *going to do*—only something you've already done. It is over. It is finished. It is the past. Success moves forward, and accomplishment looks back.

That doesn't mean that successful people don't accomplish things. They do, but successful people are those who understand the value of failure and its place in their lives, so they do not rest upon their laurels. They are still moving forward in life—not boasting about past accomplishments. If you think about it, no great man or woman in the Bible ever got to the place of success without first laying a foundation of failures that gave them the tools to overcome their own weaknesses.

Failure is where strength, understanding, insight, and motivation is born and also where humility can be found. People who never fail and always accomplish are often jaded in their outlook on life. They feel entitled and expect others to treat them that way. People who worked hard and failed over and over often come out the other side with an appreciation for others and the struggles most people go through to succeed. This journey of failure brings a sense of humility and appreciation for others.

The Bible only uses the word *success* one time. The word is found in Joshua 1:8 where God said to Joshua, "This book of the law shall not depart out of thy mouth; but thou shalt meditate therein day and night, that thou mayest observe to do according to all that is written therein: for then thou shalt make thy way prosperous, and then thou shalt have good success." Within that verse is an implicit understanding that success will not come easily, but will be a daily struggle—one that is filled with constant failures and mishaps. Joshua's job wasn't to succeed. His job was to push forward each and every day despite any setbacks, and in doing so, he would find success.

In verse 7, God told Joshua the goal: "That thou mayest observe to do according to all the law, which Moses my servant commanded thee: turn not from it to the right hand or to the left, that thou mayest prosper whithersoever thou goest." Verse 8 then explained how Joshua could attain that goal—by meditating on God's Word day and night. Success wasn't something Joshua was going to be able to achieve by strength of his will or might. He would have to work at it each and every day.

Real men are those who see failure as an opportunity to grow and expand their horizons—not as an excuse to quit or stagnate. Part of manhood is accepting failure as a normal part of life and to see it as the growing opportunity that it is. No child ever simply stands up one day and walks for the first time as if he had done it for years. To learn to walk first requires a lot of falling down. In fact, learning to fall right is a fantastic skill to have. But failure upon failure eventually leads to successful walking, running, and jumping.

The Bible says, "For a just man falleth seven times, and riseth up again: but the wicked shall fall into mischief."[30] The only difference between the just man and the wicked man in that proverb is that when the just man falls, he gets back up. His failure becomes the drive to get back up and try again. A wicked man falls into mischief and is snared therein. His failure becomes his excuse.

A man's path to successful manhood is paved with failure.

## Failing at What I Loved to Do

Growing up, I read a lot. I loved reading, and I became engrossed in science fiction and fantasy novels—perhaps not the best reading habits, but better than many others. Having loved the books I read, I began to have a desire to write my own novel when I was a freshman in high school. At this time, I lived in Greensboro, North Carolina, and attended a local high school.

I began writing a fantasy novel with the belief that I would get it published and become "famous." During that year, I met Randy, a sophomore in high school. He too loved fantasy and science fiction, and once he found out I was writing a novel, he

---

[30] Proverbs 24:16

asked to collaborate with me. So we became co-authors on this project.

However, Randy was a superior writer, and I soon began to feel inadequate. My grammar and spelling, sorry to say, was atrocious, my prose lacked imagination, and I struggled to grasp some of the core techniques of fictional writing. I'm sure at times Randy felt frustration with me, and one time we had a day long fight over the use of the word "pity" in the book.

For three years, Randy and I wrote on this book. After my freshman year, I moved back to Arizona, but I flew back to North Carolina the next two summers to spend about a month to a month and a half with Randy while we continued to work on our book. When finished, we were extremely pleased with the outcome. We had finished our first novel, containing around 120,000 words—quite an accomplishment for two high schoolers.

We printed out the whole thing, boxed it, and sent it to a publisher. Weeks later, we received the entire manuscript back with a nicely worded letter that basically said our work did not meet their needs at that time. Translation: it's not that good of a story, you don't write that well, and we wouldn't be able to sell it, so we're going to pass on it.

That rejection letter was incredibly disappointing and a major blow to our pride and egos. During my senior year in high school back in Gilbert, Arizona, I took an AP English class. I thought with all my experience in writing a 120,000-word novel that this class would be a walk in the park. But I vividly recall my teacher's becoming increasingly frustrated over my lack of grammar skills. My essays would be returned to me filled with red ink to fix grammar and spelling issues.

I grew increasingly insecure in my ability to write. I thought my essays were good, thoughtful, and insightful, but the content always seemed to be lost in a sea of red correction ink. No matter what I wrote, the way I wrote it supposedly distracted the reader from the real content. I really struggled in that class. I couldn't please the teacher no matter what I did. In fact, he lectured me in front of the whole class—or at least they couldn't help but to overhear—about a basic grammar issue I repeatedly failed to get right.

"Greg," he said, his voice bubbling with exasperation, "what's the matter with you? When you use the article 'a,' you always write 'an' when preceding a noun that starts with a vowel. It's 'an apple,' not 'a apple.' This is basic stuff. You should've learned this rule long ago!"

For a guy who wanted to be a writer, this public correction was humiliating. I had thoughts of sharing my novel with him, but after all that, I dared not. I was scared he would just laugh at me. Clearly, he thought I shouldn't be in his AP class—not with such grammatical and spelling deficiencies as I possessed.

But I continued to write anyway. I wrote and wrote. In Bible college, I wrote fairytale-like stories about my girlfriend and eventual wife, Liberty. I even used such a story to propose to her! I tried to get other things published, but never could. I received rejection letter after rejection letter.

I gradually improved. My failures only spurred me on to do better, to learn more, to be a better writer. It wasn't until my mid-thirties that a publisher finally picked up my one of my books, *Fitly Spoken*. Strangely, it wasn't even a novel. It was a book on Christian principles for building good communication skills. Ironic, eh?

Since then, I've had several more books published, including my first novel when I was nearly forty years of age! It wasn't the novel I wrote in high school. It wasn't any of the many other books

I'd written since then, but it was the accumulation of the many things I'd learned from failure after failure of trying to get a novel published.

As of this writing, I am not only continuing to write and publish books, but I am also an experienced editor—if only my English teacher could see me now! My failures only helped me to better myself. I don't know if I'm naturally talented in writing or not—my teacher would claim I am not—but having allowed my failures to be my motivator, I have become a successful writer.

That is how manhood deals with failure. There is always more to learn from failure than from success, but failure is only good when we do actually learn something from it. Take failure and use it. Learn from it. Let it push you toward success.

Son, what do you think you are a failure at? Is it possible that your failure will make you into a better man than any accomplishment your talent or skill may bring?

## No One Wants to Hire a Cripple

My freshman year of Bible college was not the most enjoyable year of my life. I never really thought of quitting, but I never saw that year as one of resounding success. To be frank, I was still growing up. Leaving home didn't make me an adult, though it helped make an adult out of me.

Bro. Tally was in charge of student placement for off-campus employment. In other words, he helped students find jobs. Back then, the easiest job to get was with UPS, a back-breaking, labor-intensive job of moving and sorting boxes into and out of trucks at one of UPS's transfer hubs in Chicago. Most of the men who came to the college as freshmen ended up being referred to UPS, and since UPS had a high turnover rate, they greedily snapped up as many of the college students as they could.

I had back problems and have had them for most my life. When as a kid, I remember my back going out of place during a jump-roping contest at school. On another occasion, I put my back out of place simply by bending over on the floor to work on some old computers. I knew I had this issue, so working at UPS did not appeal to me at all. I figured I needed to make Bro. Tally aware of this fact so he could help me find a job that would not be so hard on my back. I had other skills. I could type very fast, and I knew my way around computers—surely there were jobs where these skills could be utilized.

So I made the expected appointment to go see Bro. Tally. When I walked in, he waved me to a chair. Bill Tally was a large man and talked with a drawl. "UPS is hiring," he said without preamble. "Here's an application."

He shoved a stapled packet of papers across his desk toward me. I looked at it, but didn't take it. "Sir, I've had a back problem since I was a kid. Doing the job they require is just going to injure my back. I'm afraid I won't be able to do it for very long. Is there another job I could get? I can—"

"Get up, son," he ordered gruffly, cutting me off from saying anything further. He pulled himself up out of his own chair, walked to his office door, and opened it. "Get out of here. No one wants to hire a cripple."

I flushed, not sure if I should be angry or ashamed. I couldn't retract my words, and clearly he assumed I was just a lazy lout looking for a plush job. No doubt he believed I wouldn't last very long in college and so figured he'd save me and some company the dubious pleasure of ever meeting.

"But—" I tried to protest.

"Get out of here. I'm busy."

Feeling both shame and anger now, I slinked out of his office. I certainly felt like a failure at that moment. I did have a job before I came to him, but I'd been let go because I couldn't get behind what the company was trying to sell. I came to Bro. Tally because everyone said he was the man I should talk to, that he had all sorts of jobs lined up. But Bro. Tally only offered me the one job I felt I couldn't do well—or at least for any length of time. He wouldn't even give me the time of day or even consider my situation.

Embarrassed, angry, and feeling depressed, I decided to find something on my own. I'd show him. But my efforts didn't go so well. For the next two years, I bounced from job to job. I tried selling picture packages back before digital cameras were even invented. That didn't go so well. I made a terrible salesman. I went from that to trying to sell Kirby vacuums, which also ended in disaster. I tried cleaning carpets, but that was only part-time work, and I was only needed sporadically for that job.

My next job was working for TruGreen ChemLawn calling people from a list and trying to sell them a package for lawn applications. I had already failed at a job like this, and so found it very trying. I couldn't make the sales expected of me. Over the summer, they let me help with the actual tree and shrub trimming services, but that assignment was temporary. Eventually, they couldn't find a place for me and let me go—mostly because I couldn't make the sales they required. I'm telling you, telemarketing is my bane.

I did land a job all on my own working as a bill of lading processor for a trucking company. That job at least utilized my skills with a computer, but the work environment was atrocious. I worked only with women who took perverse joy in pointing out every mistake I made and insisting on playing some of the most horrid music I'd ever heard in my life. I tried to resist, but ultimately my supervisor fired me because of performance issues. I blamed those witches—at least that is how I thought at the time—and found myself once again unemployed.

For two years, I'd tried on my own to remain gainfully employed and ended up failing at everything I tried. I barely had my head above water financially, and I was too embarrassed and prideful to call my parents for help—not that they could help me anyway. My dad had been embezzled out of a significant amount of money, and he was in no position to help me even if I asked.

Finally, with no other option available to me, I swallowed my pride and went back to see Bro. Tally. I remembered vividly what he had said to me two years earlier. I remembered the feeling I had when he kicked me out of his office. I'd not spoken to the man since and had studiously avoided him. But left with few options, I went to see him.

I ambushed him out in the parking lot since I couldn't find him in his office. "Bro. Tally, my name is Greg Baker. I recently got let go from my job and was wondering if you have anything I could look into."

He paused and studied me, frowning deeply. I wondered if he remembered who I was. "What year are you?" he asked.

"Junior, sir."

"Hmmm." He rubbed his chin. "I might have something at that. I just got a call from UGN. They're hiring. I told them I'd send a couple upperclassmen. Would you be interested?"

This time, I didn't care what the job was. I didn't even ask. "Absolutely!"

I got the job and worked there for the next three years before heading off to Colorado to pastor.

In retrospect, I think Bro. Tally gave me the job opportunity because I was still in college despite my failures. I believe he had fully expected me to quit and leave the college, but my failure had taught me some valuable lessons. Each time I failed, I had learned a little about myself and matured as a result. My failures helped make me understand work ethic in ways I'd never before understood. When I left UGN to go pastor, I left a company that wanted me to stay on. They even offered me an additional raise to do so. That was a far cry from all those other jobs at which I had failed.

Failure is a much better teacher than success is. The experience matured me in ways that success could never do. Instead of using my failure as an excuse to quit, I pressed on and used my failures to improve my character.

Son, you will do that too. You will fail, and when you do, you will either use that failure as an excuse or use it as a tool to learn and improve.

# CHAPTER NINE

# A Patient Man Is a Perfect Man

Patience is not waiting. Just because someone waits for something doesn't mean that he waited patiently. An online dictionary summarizes *patience* as "the ability to tolerate delay, trouble, or suffering without getting upset or angry." Patience, as defined in this way, is an ability. The Bible, however, indicates that patience is much, much more than a mere ability.

Interestingly, along with wisdom, patience is personified in the Bible. In other words, patience is given human characteristics and even a feminine pronoun: "But let patience have *her* perfect work, that ye may be perfect and entire, wanting nothing."[31] According to the Bible, patience is more than an ability; it is a work, a force, that is done in us—that can only exist when we must endure something difficult.

The verses right before the one quoted, say, "My brethren, count it all joy when ye fall into divers temptations; Knowing this, that the trying of your faith worketh patience."[32] To be joyful when

---

[31] James 1:4.
[32] James 1:2-3.

we fall into difficult times is odd. Most people don't get excited when faced with difficult or uncertain times. But James, the author of these verses under the inspiration of God, understood that patience itself is a force that brings about a significant change in a man.

When we endure difficult times, our character is put through a series of tests designed to grow us, change us, and improve us. A patient man is a perfect man. He does not lack anything in his character. He will not become angry. He will not lose his temper. He will not get desperate enough to become foolish. He has foresight. He exhibits understanding. He is willing to see things from others' points of view. These are the qualities, among others, that patience can bring to the table of a man's character.

Romans chapter 5 agrees with this analysis of patience. In Romans, we see a progression that starts with tribulation and leads to patience and then to what patience can give to a man.

1. We are to glory in tribulation (Romans 5:3)
2. Because tribulation brings patience (Romans 5:3)
3. And patience then brings experience (Romans 5:4)
4. And experience ultimately brings hope (Romans 5:4)

The experience spoken of here only proves that God can give us what we need to survive the tribulation. God uses patience to build our character so that we can weather these trials of life, and once you know this, there is hope (strong confidence) of weathering the next one. Patience is what brings this experience— this honing of one's character.

James speaks of the patience of Job,[33] but Job endured some of the most traumatic events any human can suffer. If you study the book of Job, he did more than endure. He learned. He grew. He became more. This is the patience to which James refers. It isn't that Job outlasted God or Satan, but he became something more. At the end, Job saw God in a way he never before could. He understood God in a way he never before could have.[34]

You see, until that point, Job had become bitter about the trials he faced. He did not believe God was right in allowing those evil things to happen to him. But when he accepted his situation, patience changed him into a better man.

Patience always involves a degree of acceptance. If you fight the situation, believing it is not fair, that you are being treated unjustly by others or even God, then you are not allowing patience to do a work in you. A man must accept the situation in life in which he finds himself. He cannot live in denial or anger. Regardless of the reasons that brought about the trial, the trial itself will not go away because you wish it to. Once you accept it, you can glory in the trial and allow patience to remold your character and person into a better man.

## Accepting Defeat

During the time I pastored in Greeley, Colorado, our church had the opportunity to purchase a new building. We were growing, and the tiny building we were in was homey, but very limited. I felt we needed to move into a larger facility. We hunted around until we found a building that would suit our needs.

---

[33] James 5:11.
[34] Job 42:1-6.

We prayed and honestly felt that this was God's will. The only obstacle was the city. The city had an ordinance that any two-story, commercial building must have a fire suppressant sprinkler system installed. The building we were trying to purchase was technically only a single story that sat atop its own parking lot. The structure had been built on a second-story level, which was enough to cause the building inspector and the fire chief to demand that we first install this costly sprinkler system.

The entire system would have cost nearly $50,000—way too much money for our little church. The only way the church family could move into this facility would be if the building inspector and fire chief both signed off and waived this requirement. They were nice guys, but sticklers for keeping to building codes—which, in retrospect, was right for them to do. However, they now stood between God's will and our church. In a way, they became the enemy—the big, mean city of Greeley trying to squash God's church!

So I determined to pray and get God to divinely change their minds. I spent hours at the building, walking through every square foot of the place and dedicating it to the Lord's purpose. I took off my shoes and walked and prayed. I spent all night in prayer in the spot where the pulpit was to be. I said things like, "God, this is not my building, and it's not the city of Greeley's building. This is Your building. This building will be used for Your honor and Your glory. Lives will be changed here…souls will be saved. Please, dear God, change their minds! Do not let them hinder Your work. Rebuke Satan. Build a hedge around this place and use it for Your glory."

The next day, I met with the chief building inspector of Greeley and the fire chief. Confident that God would answer my prayers, I walked them through the building and showed them our architectural plans. We convened in the foyer. "Well, gentlemen, that's the plan. What do you think?"

They looked at each other, and the building instructor said, "I still can't sign off on this without the suppression system in place."

I stiffened and silently rebuked Satan. "Technically, this is not a two-story building," I explained. "It shouldn't need the system. Many other buildings larger than this one do not."

He shook his head. "Doesn't matter. I understand what you're saying, but the structure is still not on ground level." He looked at the fire chief for confirmation. "One of the reasons the code is in place is because getting out of structures like this is harder. Having stairs to navigate is one reason why we want the suppression system in place so any fires can be extinguished more quickly."

The fire chief nodded. "He's right. I can't sign off on this either."

With my hackles up, I proceeded to argue with the two of them. My arguments were sound. They were logical. The city was being unreasonable. Their codes were ludicrous and not applicable in this situation. Both men dug their heels in and resisted. They refused to budge.

I couldn't believe it! All that praying for nothing. All that hope for nothing. All that effort for nothing!

About that time, I came to accept the situation. I didn't blame Satan. I didn't blame God. I didn't blame the city of Greeley. I just accepted that we were not going to be able to get that building. It was just the way it was, and I had better start dealing with reality instead of being angry that things were not going according to my plans.

The moment I accepted the situation, patience did a work in my heart, and I felt at peace. It didn't matter if we got the building or not. God was still in control, and serving Him didn't hinge on whether we met in that building or in a park somewhere.

I nodded to the two men and let a genuine smile cross my face. "Okay," I said, "if you can't, you can't. I appreciate you both coming out here. It means a lot that you took the time to do this yourself when you could have just sent someone."

I reached out to shake the fire chief's hand, but he stepped back, a thoughtful expression on his face. He said, "However, I think there might be a way I could sign off on this." He turned to the building inspector, ignoring my hand. "What if they only use half the building and install a monitored fire alarm system? Since the maximum occupancy would be greatly reduced, I think that would be sufficient, don't you?"

Half the building was unfinished anyway. Our intention was to start in the half that was finished and grow to the point where we could expand into the other side. Even the half that was finished was quite a bit larger than the building we currently possessed. Since this proposal fit our plans anyway, my eyes lit up in wonder.

The building inspector gave it a moment's thought and slowly nodded. "I think I could sign off on that."

And the obstacle was removed—just like that.

Perhaps the main obstacle in the situation was not Satan, not the inspector, not the fire chief, not the city of Greeley, but me. When I surrendered to the situation and accepted it, I was able to truly turn it over to the Lord. I, as a person, grew in that moment of patience. I became a better pastor, a better man.

We should pray. We should claim God's promises. We should call upon God's power and might. But sometimes there must be acceptance of the situation in which you find yourself. It might be that God has allowed the trial into your life. You need to meet it with patience and come out the other side as a perfect man.

## Patience, You Turkey!

My uncle called me "Turkey" though I don't know why. He lived on a farm in eastern Indiana, and occasionally he actually did have turkeys—they were mean buzzards, let me tell you! I distinctly recall a girl being attacked by one of those monstrosities, so I just couldn't see the connection between me and that mean-tempered bird.

On one of our family trips to his farm, I discovered that he had some old silver dimes from the 1920s. I'd recently gotten into a coin-collecting phase, and so those silver dimes were a treasure I dearly coveted. My uncle was not married, and though he did marry late in life, he had no children of his own. His nieces and nephews were the closest thing he had to children, so I think he felt toward us boys as any other father might. Regardless, it wouldn't have stopped me from asking if I could have a few.

"Uncle Ralph," I whispered, eyes wide and fixed on the coins, "can I have some?"

He regarded me thoughtfully. "Whatever for?"

"I've started my own coin collection. These would be great to have."

"Oh? What is it that you've collected?"

"Mostly pennies, but I'd like to start collecting many of the others...like dimes."

He tsked, knowing perfectly well that I was trying to manipulate him. "I'll think about it," he promised.

We wouldn't be leaving for another four days, but I really, really had my heart set on those dimes. "When?" I demanded.

"When what?"

"When will you think about it?"

He tsked again. "Patience, Turkey! You'll just have to be patient."

At my young age, maybe seven or eight, being patient was not something I did well. In fact, I thought having patience to be merely a copout for not making the decision. What was the point in waiting? Why couldn't I know right then? What difference would it make?

That evening, maybe four hours later—an eternity in my opinion—I asked again. "Uncle, did you think about it?"

He let out one of his patented tsks and shook a finger at me. "You're going to have to be patient, Turkey. I'll let you know when I've decided."

I tried everything to hasten him along, but he was stubborn in his own right, and eventually I gave up. Just before we left to return to Arizona, he brought out the dimes and took out perhaps ten of them. "Did we learn anything about patience?" he asked, grinning broadly as he held the coins.

I just knew he was going to give them to me, so I lied, "Yes." I hadn't learned a thing. I was just as impatient as ever.

"What did you learn?"

I had to think fast. "Sometimes you have to wait."

Perhaps it wasn't the best answer, but it was a good enough answer for a kid, I guess. He handed over the coins to my greedy hands. "Remember this," he said, "and learn some patience."

I have remembered my uncle's lesson. Even though I didn't learn much about patience at the time, the circumstances have stuck with me through the years. There are times when we must wait, but not for waiting's sake. It could be that we must wait on God's answer to our prayers so that He can do a work in our lives. It could be we must wait on the next stage in life until we are prepared. Even though I didn't learn much at such a young age, the memory did stick with me and did me good stead in later years.

Patience, even forced patience, did a work in me that made me a better man. Sometimes we want everything in life to come to us when we think it should. We want the perks in life without any of the time and effort that should be paid first. So often you learn more while you wait than you do at any other time. It might be why God said three times to "wait on the Lord."[35]

Son, what is it in your life that you are being forced to wait on? What can you learn during this time of forced patience that might make you a better man someday?

## Wrestling Match with a 2000-Pound Bertha

In my freshman year of college, my uncle decided to gift me with a car. That was exciting! I only had to pay one dollar for the vehicle, and even a poor college student could do that. I remember envisioning a sleek-looking vehicle that would be the envy of everyone on campus. When my uncle was telling me about it, I thought he'd said he was giving me a Chevy Cavalier. The new

---

[35] Psalms 27:14; Psalms 37:34; Proverbs 20:22.

models of the early 1990s looked pretty sweet. A Cavalier wasn't a luxury car, but it wouldn't embarrass me either.

The truth was something altogether different. I took a Greyhound bus to Liberty, Indiana, where my uncle picked me up and took me to his farm. There he introduced me to "Bertha." At that point in time, Bertha didn't actually have a name, but my roommate, Jake, christened the car that later in the year. Henceforth, my memory will always attribute the name of Bertha to this beast of a car that my uncle gave me.

This was no Chevy Cavalier. In fact, my "envy of the campus" was a white, 4-door, hatchback, 1983 Chevy Chevette. Nothing about the vehicle was sleek or terribly attractive, but the body style was not what I saw at first. Smack-dab in the center of the roof was a yellow emergency light seen on top of city work-crew vehicles. That light looked so out of place that I needed a moment to register the fact that it was a permanent part of the car! Apparently, the car had been an old telecommunication's vehicle used by Ameritech, the local phone company.

That light even worked! A switch had been installed on the dashboard that when flicked, the light on top turned on, spun, and flashed! Oooh…I'd certainly be the envy of everyone at school! Right. I almost turned it down on the spot, but hey, it was a free car. Guess I could *endure* this eyesore if I didn't have to beg for rides to work or even to get a haircut.

Bertha and I didn't have an amicable relationship. She was feisty, to say the least. College students, of course, always have plenty of money to spend on fixing up cars—at least that is what Bertha must've thought, for she certainly did everything in her power to get me to spend what I had.

The repairs began when the tailpipe rusted through right at the manifold. So now, not only did my car look like a thing of envious beauty what with that conspicuous yellow light on top, but she began sounding like some sort of injured, pain-crazed monstrosity that could be heard several city blocks away—just what I wanted when pulling out of the college parking lot.

Jake wasn't overly pleased either since I was his ride to work. We both worked at TruGreen ChemLawn in Crestwood, Illinois, and since he didn't want to be stared at the entire way to work, he determined to jerry-rig it, seeing as I didn't have the money to get the tailpipe properly replaced. We took several Arizona Ice Tea cans because they were longer than a normal soda can, emptied out the tea, cut off the ends, split them down the middle, and wrapped them around the tailpipe and the connection to the manifold. We then took two hose clamps and tightened it all together.

Our splice worked! For a time. We could go perhaps three days like that before the heat tore a hole right through the aluminum cans, and Bertha started her unseemly belching again. So about every three or four days, we would spend twenty minutes replacing the patch with new Arizona Ice Tea cans. Trust me, that splicing grew old real fast.

Then Bertha really tried to test my patience. While Jake was driving to work on Interstate 80/294 in South Chicago, Bertha blew a tire. I was actually sitting in the passenger seat reading my Bible. Dominic, a fellow college student who worked with us, was fast asleep in the back, draped over the seat. We were in the leftmost speed lane and traveling nearly 70 mph when the rear tire on the driver's side blew out without any warning whatsoever.

I heard a pop and looked up in time to watch as Bertha failed to turn with the road, and we slammed into the concrete barriers that often line freeways. Perhaps because the road was turning or perhaps because of the center of gravity of the car allowed it,

Bertha climbed the concrete barriers on two wheels, and we were launched into the air sideways.

Time does interesting things in such instances, and for a long moment, time slowed way down. My Bible disappeared even as my face slammed against the passenger window. I remember looking out the window at the ground below and seeing debris flash by. I looked straight up at Jake who was staring down at me with an expression that shouted, "It's not my fault!"

Bertha must not have been completely sideways, for she came down on top of the concrete barrier which, strangely, knocked her back onto the road where she landed on all four tires. Time sped up again as we immediately began slamming bodily into the concrete barrier on our left.

"You got it, Jake!" I yelled encouragingly as he wrestled for control of Bertha.

And that's when Dominic, who wasn't wearing a seatbelt, woke up in the back. I don't know how, perhaps g-forces and the friction of being draped over the backseat kept him in place, but he was still sitting there despite being in a car that had been tossed into the air sideways. He woke up and yelled, "Bro! Hit the brakes!"

Jake, purely out of reflex, slammed on the brakes. Not good.

Time slowed down again as Bertha did a 180 through all four lanes of interstate traffic. It was like some sort of scary version of dodge ball. We slid in behind a semi-truck as it sped on past, blaring its horn. We slid into another lane only to see an approaching car barreling down upon us, missing us by inches as we slid out of the way and into the next lane.

Miraculously, we hit no one, but went through all four lanes and slammed into the guard railing on the other side of the freeway, facing oncoming traffic.

Time returned to some semblance of normalcy. All three of us sat there for a moment, trying to determine if we'd really survived all of that in one piece. I needed air—fresh air—even the smog-tainted air of the freeway. I jumped out of the car and stood there trembling with relief and reaction, gulping in air by the truckload.

Only one car stopped; no one else even slowed down. The man in the car, an off-duty traffic officer, came running up to me.

"You guys okay?" he demanded, his eyes a bit wild, probably much like mine.

I poked my head back in the car. "You guys okay?" I echoed. Jake nodded and Dominic said something as he climbed out of the car himself. It didn't register, but he seemed okay enough. I pulled my head back out. "We're fine," I told the officer.

He stood there for a moment looking at us as if he couldn't really believe we were fine. He then said, "You have no idea what that car just did."

I nodded. "Oh yes, I do." Every bit of it had been seared forever in my brain. We, no doubt, had crushed a dozen angels during that fiasco. Regardless, I was praising God for our miraculous survival.

Jake got out, and we took stock of Bertha. One tire was blown, and in the examination, the only thing we could find wrong with the tire was a puncture high up on the wheel wall. That seemed odd. It looked more like a bullet hole than a typical blowout. The other tires, all of them in fact, had bulges from where they either scrapped along the ground when we were sideways or against the concrete barrier along the freeway. Both of the front tires, however, were bent inward at the top and sticking outward at the bottom. That didn't look good. The whole front end was a mess, and even good tires couldn't last long with that sort of crazy alignment. The only other damage, strangely, was a broken taillight when we slammed into the guard railing after having crossed all lanes of traffic at once.

The officer asked Jake, "Would you like to fill out an accident report?"

I did not. The reason was because I didn't have any insurance. I had dropped the insurance when I could no longer afford it, so I'd been driving without it for a month or so. I shook my head at Jake, who eyeing me strangely, said, "No. Guess not. I think we'll just try to get to work."

The officer looked at the bulges evident on the remaining tires. "You're not going to make it," he predicted.

We didn't have much of a choice but to try. We changed the blown tire for the spare, and despite the spare's awkward appearance, it was now the best tire on the car.

"You want to drive?" Jake asked before getting back in.

Bertha belonged to me, but I didn't want to drive. No sir. So I used logic to get out of it. "You'd better do it. After something like that, you don't want to get gun shy."

I don't think Jake wanted to drive either, but he gave in and we got in. We started her up and then sat there looking out the front window. There was a problem. We were facing the wrong way. Traffic zoomed by us, and we could see no opportunity to make a U-turn in the middle of the interstate.

So I reached over and flipped the switch that turned on the yellow emergency light on top of the roof. Finally! I got some use out of the thing. "You'll have to drive backwards to an on ramp," I told Jake.

"Yeah." He didn't appear enthusiastic.

So, putting Bertha in reverse and with a yellow light flashing atop the sorry-looking car of mine, we backed up about a half mile to an on ramp where we successfully made a backwards U-turn. Keeping the light on, we merged with traffic and drove gingerly and apprehensively toward the city of Crestwood and work. At any moment, we expected another tire to blow or the engine to stop.

We sat on pins and needles, praying fervently for mercy and grace to get us to work before something else went wrong. At last, we pulled into the parking lot at work. Jake parked Bertha off to the side out of the way, knowing we'd have to do some work before we could get her back to the college. We rolled to a stop, and Jake turned off the ignition. He then reached up and patted the dashboard. "Good girl, Bertha."

Just then, the front driver tire blew with a loud pop. Bertha seemed to sag in exhaustion with Jake's hand still resting on the dashboard.

The comic relief was too much to endure. Jake and I tumbled out of the car, roaring with laughter and relief. Dominic ran off, no doubt to tell everyone at work what had happened, but Jake and I just rolled on the ground, laughing uncontrollably. The whole episode, every bit of it, just struck us as odd.

But Bertha wasn't done with me. I got four used tires to replace the damaged ones, and I even took it to a muffler shop where the tailpipe was replaced and welded to the manifold so that I no longer needed the Arizona Ice Tea cans. That was nice. After picking it up from the shop one afternoon, I drove off to work feeling pretty good about my situation. The fact that the tires still didn't ride correctly would require some serious work in order to fix, but at least I didn't feel I was driving around in a belching dragon any longer.

On the freeway, Bertha once again tested my patience. A pickup truck ahead of me hit a bump and a huge block of wood, probably two feet square, fell out and hit the road right in front of me. I hit it hard, running around sixty miles per hour, and just ran it over.

The impact rattled every bone in my body. Shaken, I hastily pulled over and took stock. The oil pan was damaged and was leaking oil something fierce. In addition, the block of wood had destroyed my brand-new tailpipe, sheering the back part of it off and knocking it loose from its mounting brackets. The sharp end had swung over and was carving a grove in my new tire.

Oh how I hated that car! It seemed as if the entire universe was conspiring to make my car-owning experience an unmitigated disaster. I jerked the pipe away from the tire, found something to tie it back so it wouldn't completely destroy my tire, and then got back in. I determined to make an end of it. I'd sell Bertha. I had had enough of that car. I just wanted to get to work and then back to the college. I determined I'd get a new car, and Bertha could rust away the rest of her existence in some forgotten junkyard.

But I didn't quite make it to work. The block of wood had done more damage than I supposed. So while on Cicero Avenue, the timing chain slipped, and I found myself in the wrong lane with a car that literally was going nowhere. I managed to coast to a stop in the turning lane between the north and southbound lanes. At this point, I wanted to cuss. I'd have dearly loved to take a wrecking ball to the infernal machine and see its parts scattered through several unrelated counties.

Someone took pity on me and helped me push Bertha across the busy street and into a parking lot of a strip mall. There, I took off the license plate, took out my registration, and any other information that could easily identify the car as belonging to me, and said goodbye. I walked away from Bertha and never once looked back.

But the test of my patience wasn't finished yet, and Bertha had the last laugh. I felt like I absolutely still needed a car. Finding rides to places was like pulling teeth. I often had to pay people for rides, and few wanted to take time out of their schedule to drag me around to places. I felt like a car was a necessity, so despite Bertha's betrayal, I still needed to get another car. I traded in Bertha on another car from a used dealership, but since Bertha was sitting in a parking lot in another city about an hour's drive away, the dealer cut my trade-in value down to practically nothing to pay for the tow. I wasn't please, but I had a new, used car, so as long as I never had to lay my eyes on Bertha again, it was worth it.

Less than a week later, I was returning from a visit with my uncle, when this new car suddenly lost a significant amount of power on the interstate. My mother had come up from Arizona for a visit, and we were returning together to the college when it happened. I pulled over, and that's when I noticed the billowing smoke pouring from my engine. The radiator hose had come loose, causing the engine to overheat, destroying the head gasket and ruining one or two of the pistons. No warning light had come on to warn me of the problem, and no temperature gauge had alerted me of the issue either.

I couldn't believe it. Nothing was going right. I limped home and returned the car to the dealership. After dickering with him for a time about selling me a lemon in which he blamed the problem on me, we eventually agreed to return the car to him, and I'd just be out my down payment...which was only a couple hundred dollars.

By then, I had had enough of cars. Begging for rides had to be a lot easier than dealing with the woes of car ownership. God taught me some valuable lessons through all that. Despite my feelings on the issue, God proved that I really didn't need another car. I managed to get around anyway, and though having a car would have been convenient, I still went an entire year after that without one—and survived. My impatience to get another car led me into making a bad decision. I didn't take the time to do the proper research or to pray. My haste in trying to fulfill a supposed need only cost me more.

Through the whole experience, I ended up with little money and no car. But I did gain something. I gained an understanding that what I really need is not necessarily what I think it is. My impatience led me down a road of desire and erroneous suppositions. God used Bertha to teach me some valuable lessons I've never forgotten.

Son, what trial in your life is God using to allow patience to do her perfect work in you?

# CHAPTER TEN
# Don't Be a Quitter

Perhaps the most insidious quality a man can possess is that of being a quitter. At the same time, one of the most destructive qualities a man can possess is not knowing when to quit. A man can form the habit of quitting, thereby marring his character to the point where he can't be trusted, can't be counted on, can't complete anything he starts, and will never know the confidence that comes with such strength of will. A man can also continue along a path of obvious self-destruction and obvious futility to the point where he destroys the things he loves because of his single-minded determination not to quit that which he should have abandoned.

The dichotomy presented in the previous paragraph shows that a balance must be found as a man. This chapter will focus on the poisonous quality of being a quitter. The next will deal with the destructive quality of not knowing when to quit.

The Scriptures teach us to "endure hardness as a good soldier."[36] Timothy uses an interesting turn of phrase because even bad soldiers often endure hardness. How you endure is what

---

[36] 2 Timothy 2:3.

makes the difference. It is the mindset that you have a job to do and nothing will stop you from doing the job and doing it well.

A real man doesn't quit because things get tough. He doesn't quit because things don't go his way. He doesn't quit when he faces setbacks. He doesn't quit in the face of the enemy. He pushes on, knowing that the act of moving forward is both good and holy. Even if he never reaches his objective, he is not found to cower or to have shown his back. He is a man. And he doesn't quit.

Paul claims he "pressed toward the mark for the prize of the high calling of God."[37] He pushed forward to reach the finish line. Whether he is in first place or last place doesn't matter. He isn't pushing forward to beat others, but to finish. The prize he speaks of isn't given to whoever finishes first. The prize *is* the mark. The prize is gained in the finishing and not by quitting. Paul verified this fact when he told Timothy, "I have fought a good fight, I have finished my course, I have kept the faith: Henceforth there is laid up for me a crown of righteousness, which the Lord, the righteous judge, shall give me at that day: and not to me only, but unto all them also that love his appearing."[38]

Perhaps Paul's greatest fear was that of becoming a castaway[39]—someone who has quit the fight and is no longer a soldier for Christ. He did not want to become a castaway for the cause of Christ. In contrast, Paul claimed that his greatest quality was not his preaching, not his charisma, not his intelligence, but his work ethic. In other words, he just didn't quit. He "laboured more abundantly than they all."[40]

---

[37] Philippians 3:14.
[38] 2 Timothy 4:7-8.
[39] 1 Corinthians 9:27.
[40] 1 Corinthians 15:10.

Perhaps the most useful quality a man can possess is the determination to push on regardless of the obstacles seeking to keep him from doing what he should do. This quality will take a man further in life than any skill or talent he possesses. Not being a quitter is the one quality that even your enemies will admire.

## Game Over! Might as Well Quit!

I must have been ten or eleven years old when my soccer team, the South Bank United, played for third place in the annual Thanksgiving Soccer Tournament. We'd already lost a game that had put us into this third-place match, and our morale was low. We had lost that other game, but we thought we should've won if it wasn't for what we felt like were bad calls and bad no-calls by the referee. As a result, we were playing listlessly, not giving our best in this third-place match.

With five minutes left in the game, we were down 2 to 0. I played center striker, and it seemed like I had stood on the midfield line for most of the game while the opposing team kept the ball on our side of the field. So with hardly any time left in the game, the opposing defender drifted over to where I stood kicking at the loose grass at midfield.

He said, "Guess the game is over. You might as well give up."

I'm the silent brooding type who hates confrontation, so I said nothing. But the kid's comments certainly riled me up. I seethed internally. On one hand, he was right. We'd already given up as a team. In fact, we were playing so badly that our coach had turned his back on us and was watching the game on the next field over. He'd yelled himself hoarse, along with my father, so the two of them had just turned away in disgust. We'd given up, and they knew it.

But the game still had five minutes remaining—enough time to score at least one goal and burn this pompous kid in the process. As if my thoughts had been a prayer, Jared used his oversized foot to kick the ball up and over midfield. *Breakaway!* I took off. Back then, I was fairly speedy, so I zipped by the defender and ran all the way down the field to score our first goal of the game.

Coach glanced back as the parents on our side of the field cheered. But he still was in no mood to watch, so he turned his attention back to the adjoining game.

Coach may not have been energized, but we kids were. Now we were down by only a single goal with a little over three minutes left in the game. The other team kicked off, and we attacked. I stole the ball and dribbled it down the field as fast as I could. I angled out and away from the goal, drawing several defenders with me. Then pivoting too quickly for the defenders to catch up, I centered the ball. One of my teammates intercepted the pass and kicked it toward the goal, and lo and behold, it zipped right through the goalie's legs and into the net!

Tie game!

Coach wandered back over to our sidelines after hearing us cheer again. He stood watching us with an unusual expression—a strange mixture of anger and accusation.

With fewer than two minutes left in the game, we were determined to finish it. The other team kicked off again, and we went to work. Now that we had more than a chance, I left it to my teammates to steal the ball, and I raced down the field. They did get the ball, and once again, they passed it to Jared who used that oversized foot of his to launch it down the field. I trapped it, confused my defender with a quick push in and then out and sidled past him and found a window to take a shot. I didn't waste it. The ball sailed smoothly into the upper corner of the goal out of reach of a frustrated and angry goalie.

We cheered, screamed, and came together in one of those giant group hugs where everyone piled on top of each other. In the waning minutes of the game, we pulled off an amazing comeback to win. All the frustration of having lost the other game disappeared in the victory of this game. To us, we had just won first place. That's how good a comeback-from-behind win feels. It's when you overcome what seems like insurmountable odds and when you refuse to quit and push on anyway.

Our coach hadn't said a word. He pointed to the ground, and we understood. We all sat down while he stood over us, his shadow bisecting the group of curious boys sitting before him. We'd won, so what was he going to say? I expected congratulations. I expected him to say we played hard. He said none of that.

Instead, in his deep voice that seemed to whistle over his brown mustache, he said in furious tones, "Don't ever, ever do that to me again!" He then spun on his heel and stormed off, muttering to himself.

We knew what he meant. For seventy-five minutes of the game, we'd given up. We played as if we'd already lost. Coach had yelled himself hoarse trying to motivate us and get us to play with heart. He cajoled us, berated us, and made himself into a fool in his own eyes because we'd already quit on him. We played a five-minute game, that's all. He wasn't proud that we'd won. He was furious that we hadn't played the first seventy-five minutes like we did the last five minutes. To him, we lost because we didn't deliver our best.

I appreciate his view. We boys were certainly glad we'd won the game, but years later as an adult, I see the bigger picture that our coach saw. Quitting can be contagious, and the spirit of giving up lingers. Once you start quitting, it is always easy to do it again.

## A Regretful Quitter

One of the few times I did quit something I shouldn't have still haunts me all these years later. In addition to soccer, the only other sport I played was Little League baseball—if you don't count chess. Because of the way my father's hands were, I was taught to bat left-handed even though I threw right-handed. For the most part, I did well playing baseball. One season, I was even the homerun champ, hitting more homeruns than anyone else on the team. A homerun usually meant just getting it past the outfielders.

But one season I joined a fairly good baseball team. In practice, I could hit the lights out of the baseballs, smashing them into right field with impunity, but for some reason, when it came to game time, I couldn't hit anything. I'd get so nervous and uptight that I'd strike out over and over again. Each at bat was nerve-wracking, and I hated the feeling.

Then one game, I didn't even get to play at all. I was already thinking about quitting. We were a Little League team, so the coach was somewhat under an obligation to let all the kids bat and play. In this game, I didn't even get to bat. Right before I was due up for the first time, the kid ahead of me was thrown out for our third and last out of the ballgame.

I found my mom and said, "I'm done. I want to quit. They didn't even let me play today." Honestly, what I said was just an excuse. I was already looking for a way to quit and the coaches not letting me play was my way out.

"Are you sure?" Mom asked.

"Yeah."

Mom called the two coaches over to the stands after most everyone had left. "I'm going to pull Greg from the team. He doesn't want to play anymore."

I couldn't tell if the coaches were surprised or relieved. I certainly hadn't been much of an asset to the team. The head coach looked over at me. "Why do you want to quit?"

"I didn't even get to play today. I didn't even bat."

"What? You didn't? No. You batted...didn't you?"

"No."

He hesitated, going back over the game in his mind and trying to place where I was and what I'd done. After a moment, he sighed. "I'm sorry, Greg. I didn't even realize."

But his apology didn't change anything for me. I wanted out. I hated the feelings of being the worst player on the team. I hated how my stomach churned every time I got up to bat. I hated feeling like I was letting everyone down.

So I quit.

Admittedly, I experienced a sense of relief. I no longer had to deal with those feelings, so I felt better. Unfortunately, my quitting didn't change who I was deep down. Having quit for the reasons I did only made it easier to quit later when faced with similar feelings. I taught myself that the best way to avoid these emotions that bothered me so much was to simply quit. But life doesn't work that way.

Even as an adult some thirty years later, I was still prone to these feelings. I took up softball with the men of my church, but when I showed up to my first game, I realized these guys were taking the whole thing much more seriously than I'd imagined. These weren't buddy pickup games. These were church teams with uniforms and paid umpires who played on well-maintained softball fields—and they were following the ASA softball rules. Immediately, my stomach began to churn and twist. My mouth dried up, feeling like I was chewing cotton, and I was reminded of that time all those years ago where I quit because of the exact same feeling.

I even trembled a bit the first time I got up to bat at thirty-nine years of age. I didn't quit, however, and continued to play. But I'll tell the truth. I felt like I was working through what I should've worked through when I was twelve. Having quit for purely selfish reasons all those years ago haunted me.

A man who finds it easy to quit will develop a habit of quitting. Giving up is always easier the next time. A man learns to tough out things—even when the biggest obstacle he faces is himself.

## Almost Killed by an NBA Legend

While attending Bible college to learn how to pastor, I decided that I'd better get some preaching to adults under my belt. Most of the ministry opportunities available to college students dealt primarily with children or teenagers. Working with adults was reserved for church and college staff. Still, I was determined, so I joined the jail ministry.

Every Sunday afternoon between services, a group of men—mostly in their thirties and forties—would travel to Cook County Jail in Chicago. Each of us would take a division, gather any of the inmates who wanted to attend a service in the recreation room, and preach to them. After a few months, I was given Division 8 to conduct my own services.

Division 8 at the time was the hospital division. All the people who needed some sort of medical care, including people who'd been shot or stabbed, were housed in this division. I vividly remember one guy lying on a hospital bed with four patches on his chest. "What happened to you?" I asked.

"Got shot."

I raised an eyebrow in surprise. "How many times?"

"They say four. But I only remember the first two."

Indeed. I decided to drop my line of inquiry.

These men became my congregation. I prayed for them. I studied my Bible for them. I preached to them each week. As a college freshman, I had my own little church, and I loved it. I looked forward each week to preaching to these men.

On Sunday, March 19, 1995, I arrived at the jail to find the rec room packed with inmates. I couldn't believe it. When I showed up usually only one or two inmates would be waiting in the room. I would turn off the television, which was constantly running, set up the benches for my service, and then walk around to the rooms and invite the inmates to the service. But on this Sunday, they were already there waiting for me. I felt flattered and excited all at the same time. I figured my praying had paid off. It looked to me like not a single person was left in the Division. The only other thing I incidentally noticed was that a basketball game was showing on the television.

What I didn't know was that Michael Jordan had just come out of retirement having decided that he was a better basketball player than he was a baseball player. This game was his first time playing since his so-called retirement. The inmates weren't there for me; they were there for Michal Jordan and the Chicago Bulls. Keep in mind, the majority of these men were black, and Michael Jordan was a legend among them.

Being oblivious to all of this, I did what I normally always did. I walked in and turned off the television. Yeah. That's what I did. Yep.

Before I could even welcome everyone to my church service, the entire crowd erupted into cursing and impending violence. One guy lunged at me, fists raised, and a look of pure rage stamped on his face. Shocked and surprised, I dodged—the wrong way— and backpedaled into the far corner of the room. I hopped up onto a bench and began waving my Bible in front of me like a weapon, swinging it back and forth to keep the mob at bay. I was terrified. I didn't even know what was going on or what I had done. I heard someone shout Jordan's name, and I began to put two and two together.

In desperation, I began shouting even as I brandished my Bible at them, "Who's your God anyway? Jordan or Jehovah?"

The shouting and cursing drew a few of the prison guards to the room. When they saw a skinny college white boy trapped in the corner and wielding nothing but a Bible, I guess they figured they needed to intervene. They elbowed their way to me, dragged me off the bench, put my head down, and ran me out of the room. More yelling and curses followed us out, including threats that if I ever showed back up they'd kill me or worse.

I stood in the hallway—some distance *down* the hallway— trying to get my heart out of my throat and into its normal spot. I don't think I'd ever been so scared in all my life. One inmate in a wheelchair came down the hallway. "I can't get in there anyway," he said looking wistful, "so I'll hear you preach."

So I preached my sermon to that single man in the hallway down a ways from the rec room where the rest of the inmates watched Michael Jordan play basketball.

I almost refused to go back the next Sunday. After that experience, I didn't know what to expect from those men. I had visions of newspaper headlines reading, "Skinny Preacher Kid Killed in Prison While Trying to Preach." Quitting would have been so easy. I certainly wanted to give up that ministry to Division 8. I never wanted to go through something like that again. Besides, the inmates had threatened my life if I ever came back. I didn't see any reason to give them an opportunity to make good on their threats.

But something in me wouldn't let it go at that. As scared as I was, I wasn't ready to give up just yet. I did try to get one of the other preachers to go with me, but he just waved me on with a smile and a friendly, "You'll-be-okay" comment. Not helpful.

So with dread and trepidation, I stepped into the elevator that would take me to Division 8—praying the whole way. I walked by the guard post who buzzed me into the main area and walked down the hallway toward the rec room. When I got there, I was not happy to see it full of men—not nearly as many as the previous week, but certainly more than the number who normally came to my services.

I prudently stopped in the doorway, making sure my exit wasn't blocked. This was the hospital wing. I figured I could outrun all of them if I had to.

One of the men looked up and saw me. A bright smile spread across his face. "Preacher! We was wonderin' if you'd come back!" He stood up and came over and shook my hand. "Look. We's real sorry about last week. It was wrong."

We had a great service, and several of the inmates came to trust Jesus Christ as their Saviour. Several of these men took me under their wing from then on. About three weeks later, I walked into the rec room, and a man was sitting at a small table playing cards. I didn't really mind if he played cards through my entire service, but I thought it best if I at least let him know what I was doing and invite him to hear the preaching.

"I'm Greg. I hold a service here each week. I'd like to invite you."

He looked up from his cards and sneered. "Get yer stinkin' face away from me!" He added some other unflattering words I dare not repeat.

Feeling awkward and unsure, I was worried that he would disrupt the service, so I felt the need to push the situation a bit. I stuck out my hand in an offer to shake his and said, "Well, I'm Greg. What's your name?"

He shot out of his seat as if I'd stuck a tack under him, and with my hand still outstretched, he cocked his fistfully intending to lay me out. I froze, worried that if I got in a brawl with an inmate, they'd just keep me in jail since I was already there. I also saw newspaper headlines flash in my mind that read, "Skinny Preacher Starts Riot in Prison." I decided the best thing to do would be to take it. I hoped I could turn with the punch and make it a glancing blow, but I decided blocking it would not be in my best interest.

The inmate, however, never delivered the blow. He froze, his fist still cocked, mine still out to shake his. I stood nervously, waiting for the punch. I looked into his eyes, but they weren't really focused on me. They stared at something behind me. That's when I felt the presence of someone at my back. A deep, booming voice spoke over my shoulder, "Shake the man's hand."

I glanced back and saw two huge black men standing each at one shoulder, glaring at their fellow inmate. Both of these men had gotten saved during the service after the Jordan incident. The would-be-puncher slowly lowered his fist and shook my hand.

I'm glad I didn't quit. I'm glad I stuck it out. I'm glad I endured hardness. So many blessings came as a result of just sticking it out, pushing forward even when it got tough. Quitters lose out on so many opportunities and blessings, but the man who understands this truth pushes on even if he must take a punch on the chin.

Son, what is it in your life you want to quit, but by so doing, you'd rob yourself of the many blessings and opportunities that would come if you'd just stick it out?

# CHAPTER ELEVEN
# Know When to Quit

Becoming a quitter is a blemish in a man's character that has tremendous ramifications, but just as bad, and possibly even worse, is not to know when to quit. At times quitting is the right thing to do. For example, a man should quit bad habits. He should quit any besetting sin in his life.[41] He should quit any activity that is detrimental to his family.

But such examples are obvious and should not require any more discussion. It is the less obvious times and circumstances when a man should quit that will be the focus of this chapter. When a certain direction in life is no longer good or when you clearly come to the end of what you can do, the time has come to consider quitting. Taking upon yourself more than you can handle is also possible. Scripture tells us that God "will not suffer you to be tempted above that ye are able."[42] That verse doesn't mean, however, that you cannot take on more than *you can handle* as a result of your own foolish decisions. God has given us free will, and when we exercise our will over and beyond God's will, you

---

[41] Hebrews 12:1.
[42] 1 Corinthians 10:13.

can easily take on more than you can handle. God knows what we can handle, but the height of arrogance is to presume you can handle that which is outside of God's will or beyond the ability and strength God has given you.

A man knows his limits. He knows when to cast his care upon God, and he knows when he should say no and when he should quit. He is yielded and submitted to God, but he is tender enough to know when God is moving him on to something else. That does happen. It is rare, though certainly not unheard of, for a man to stay in the same ministry, the same job, the same position for all his life. Sometimes you must quit one direction in life in order to pursue another direction that God leads you.

While playing for the Mesa Magicians, a flight one soccer team, I discovered that the level of competition and need to win games became almost all consuming to everyone involved. The coaches, in fact, went out of the way to teach little, dirty tricks to get any edge they could. They taught us to step on toes, pull on shorts, and do whatever we had to do to win. This kind of nonsense teaches the wrong lesson. Learning dirty, little tricks do not prepare kids for life—not in a right way. I quit the team because of what the coaches were teaching, and I was right to do so. At times we need to quit.

On another occasion, while swimming in the Salt River as a kid, I jumped off a large rock into a swift current and immediately tried to swim back to the rock against the current. No matter how hard I swam, I was going nowhere. If I continued on that course, I would drown. I'd bitten off more than I could chew, and for my own safety, I needed to quit and allow the current to take me downriver where I could safely make it to shore. Life is like that at times. The time may arise where swimming against the current of life means you might drown.

A man needs to know when he should let go.

## In Hot Water

My youngest son, Jacen, must have been two years old when my wife left me and our children at home so that she could run some errands in peace. So deciding to help with the housework, I went downstairs into the basement of our Greeley home to vacuum the carpet.

I was vacuuming with all the diligence of a dutiful husband when I faintly heard a strange sound that tickled my ears over the screeching of the vacuum. I hesitated a bit, listening carefully to determine if something was really out of place. I heard the sound again—a faint cry that could have been anything from a bird to a passing car. Frowning, I turned off the vacuum.

The agonizing scream of a two-year-old in mortal danger or excessive pain instantly replaced the dying noise of the vacuum. For all the world, the scream sounded as if the kid was either being eaten alive—or one of his brothers had taken away one of his toys. Honestly, sometimes it's hard to tell the difference—though moms tend to have a better innate ability to distinguish these cries of their children. Regardless, I figured I'd better check it out, so with terror-filled images flashing through my mind, I shot up the stairs.

I found Jacen standing in the bathroom sink. I'm not exactly sure how he got up there—he had to use the toilet as a stepping stool—but somehow he had not only gotten up there, but he had managed to turn on the hot water full blast and stop the sink from draining at the same time.

The poor kid stood in scalding hot water, and he couldn't get out. In the course of his adventure to the top of the sink, he'd discovered the treasures of his brothers' toothbrushes. He held tightly to these wondrous new objects as he clawed at the sink mirror in an effort to escape the hot water. Because he was holding on to those toothbrushes, he couldn't get a grip on anything else and couldn't pull himself out of the scalding water.

So he just stood in the water, screaming and clawing at the mirror in a vain attempt to escape the trap of his own making. Dad to the rescue! I snatched the kid from the water, turned off the faucet, and examined his feet. Red, but not burned—thank the Lord. That was my first relief. My second was that my wife wouldn't kill me for allowing one of her sons to be burned. (It's odd what your mind does in situations like that.)

Other than red feet and calves, my son did come away with a "prize." He still held on to his newfound treasures—the toothbrushes—in both hands. Even after all the pain, he just wouldn't let go of those toothbrushes, but if he had, he would've been able to get himself out of the sink. He didn't need to stay trapped in the hot water—if only he would have let go.

Sometimes, knowing when to let go is important. We can cling to certain things in our lives that prevent us from escaping traps of our own making. Through sheer stubbornness, we can cling to things that need to be let go. An example could be an expensive hobby, a house that you can't afford, or a girlfriend who isn't good for you. Perhaps after a sermon or some other inspiring lecture or speech, you made a declaration of what you're going to do with your life, but you misinterpreted God's leading or you were inspired to do something outside of God's will. If that is the case, you need to let it go. Perhaps you've entered a new phase of life and you need to let go of those things that are associated with the old you.

The apostle Paul said that, when he became a man, he put away childish things.[43] In other words, he quit being a child. When one phase of his life had passed, he let go of it and moved on to the next phase. Son, what do you need to let go of?

## The Hardest Thing I've Ever Done

When it comes to things you might expect to be on a list of hard things to do, quitting is not one of them. But on February 19, 2012, the hardest thing I'd ever had to do was resigning as the pastor of Gospel Light Baptist Church in Greeley, Colorado. For nearly thirteen years, I had pastored there, and to me, the people of that church had become my family.

I honestly never thought I'd step down. Over the years of pastoring, I made comments that I'd never leave—only God could make me leave. I weathered many a battle, many a difficulty, and faced my share of adversaries. Through it all, I never once thought about quitting. I wanted to serve as pastor there for the rest of my life.

About a year prior to my resignation, things began to change for me. I began to grow weary, and it seemed I was barely treading water. I felt I was going nowhere, and I felt I was not even able to take a breath. The Bible warns us not to grow weary in well-doing. The Word of God encourages us to continue on for we "shall reap if we faint not."[44] It warns that when we grow weary in well-doing, we will be prone to faint. An implicit command in the verse states that we must find ways not to grow weary in the doing of right.

---

[43] 1 Corinthians 13:11.
[44] Galatians 6:9.

A very real danger exists in being overwhelmed and overburdened. People who have been overwhelmed with serving God often burnout and have abandoned everything they claimed they once loved. Their standards change, their philosophies change, their mindset changes, and even the way they look at God changes. I've encountered people who were so burnt out on serving God that they came to hate everything Christian and anything that reminded them of Christianity—the church, the Bible, and even see their years of service to Christ as a waste. Many feel as if they have actually been cheated out of aspects of life because of their service.

To admit that I was heading down this path pains me. I did not place safeguards in my life to prevent my growing weary. I began to see the ministry as a burden and a trial to endure instead of a joy to experience. There is a difference between the two feelings in how a burden is carried. A runner who loves running will endure the hardships associated with being a successful runner simply for the pure joy of running and what it means to them. But the moment the runner sees running itself as the burden, then he is on his way out as a runner. I began seeing the ministry in such a way.

I was still praying and reading my Bible—though the burden and pressures I felt made me much less inclined to do so, and eventually I was hit and miss when it came to walking with God. My sermons were prepared haphazardly without much study. I felt relief when church was over and felt stress at the beginning of every church service and activity. I felt I needed help, but no one was in a position to give me what I needed. The church loved me and my family. I loved them. But they couldn't give me what I needed, and all too soon I could no longer give them what they needed.

The situation became untenable. My family was suffering, and I could see what the stress was doing to my wife and children. If I continued down this road, it dawned on me that I might end up being one of those people who walked away from everything. If I didn't resign from the church, I could very easily destroy many people—possibly even my own family. Getting back on track spiritually, emotionally, and mentally was not something I could do overnight. It wasn't like I could flip a switch, and everything would be all right. It would take time to heal, and I had to give myself and my family that time.

God had begun to change my vision and my heart. I realized that God understood the spiritual and mental path I was taking and was preparing to allow me to get back on track with Him. However, since it would not happen overnight, it would mean that I needed to resign. My mental and spiritual state was no longer healthy for the members of Gospel Light Baptist Church. For their sake, for mine, for my family's, and for the cause of Christ I knew I needed to step down. I needed to quit.

Continuing to pastor as I was would have been a colossal mistake. I have continued to serve God since my resignation, but if I had continued as I was, the weariness of serving would have destroyed me. I had nothing else to give. I admit my weariness was my own doing. I let things get to me that I should not have. I began to lose focus, and my time with God wasn't as sweet as it used to be. I became depressed, and my depression clung to me like a spider web or dried sweat. I couldn't shake it.

So I quit. I quit so that I wouldn't quit on God. I quit so that I wouldn't quit on my family. I quit so that the church members of Gospel Light Baptist Church could find a pastor under whom they could grow spiritually.

Stepping down from the pastorate was the hardest decision I've ever made. I am not a crier. It is just not my nature to cry, but on the Sunday I resigned, I cried publicly. I couldn't help myself. In a way, staying would have been so easy. It was what I knew, and I was receiving a paycheck—though I began to believe I did so unjustly. By resigning, I'd venture out into a brand-new world filled with its own dangers. But I needed to heal and find my equilibrium again so that I could continue serving God.

The following letter is part of my resignation statement that I read before the church on February 19, 2012:

*I, Greg Baker, am resigning as pastor of Gospel Light Baptist Church.*

*I never thought I would write those words, and it is with a heavy heart that I do so. For nearly thirteen years, I have made this city my home and the members of this church my family. It has been the honor of a lifetime to serve you, and I feel that my resignation is the best way to continue to do so. My resignation will pave the way for another man with a greater vision, greater enthusiasm, and greater ability to take you to a level that I have not been able to do.*

*I do not regret my thirteen years of service here. We have grown. People have been saved and baptized, and lives have been turned to Christ. You, more than the building or the material items contained in it, are my legacy and hope for the cause of Christianity. We have brought a light to Greeley and have made an indelible impact for the cause of Christ. Whatever direction you chose for the church, I know that I leave* behind a commodity for Christ that is worth investing in—you!

The reasons for my resignation are many, but the most important one is this: for this church to grow, to blossom into its full potential, I must step aside. Much like John the Baptist who had to diminish in order for Christ to increase, I must now do so as well. My job is finished here. I have laid a foundation in Christ and raised up a group of precious people in the Lord. I have planted, but it is now time for someone else to water. The Lord will bring the increase.

For about a year now, God has been changing my vision and heart for what I am able and capable of doing for Him. I believe He is calling me into a different phase of my ministry to Him, one that I am hopeful will impact many for Christ. I have been praying and fasting for months and have gotten counsel about this. The decision to resign is the only one that will keep both me and this church in the will of God.

The church ultimately opted to combine with another good church in area, and many, if not most, of the former members of Gospel Light Baptist Church have continued to go to church and to serve God.

Perhaps if I'd done things differently, I would still be pastoring. However, the path I found myself on made continuing to do so unwise. God's will is ultimately that each of us continue in Him, but to ensure that it happens, He might move us. This means there will be times in our lives when we must quit something so that we can continue doing right.

For some, age catches up, and carrying the load and doing all that they once did is no longer possible. The Scripture even recommends bearing a heavier yoke when you are young, implying that when you are old there will be things you'll need to quit.[45] Solomon wrote that there is a time and season to everything.[46] A season implies a beginning and an end. Times change, you change, and these changes need to be considered when deciding upon a path to walk in life.

Some things are immutable and should never be quit on, such as God, our marriage, righteousness, and decency. But learning to recognize the changing of seasons in your life and not to cling so tightly to that which is passing is important. When a season ends, we move on. When you come to the end of yourself and God's plan for something, we move on.

The key difference between a quitter and someone who knows when to quit is that a quitter doesn't move on. A quitter stagnates. A quitter looks for reasons to quit instead of looking for reasons to continue. When you look for reasons to continue and realize there are no good ones, then it may be time to let go and move on, but a quitter will never see it that way. A quitter simply looks for any reason to quit.

Son, do you look for reasons to continue or do you look for reasons to quit?

---

[45] Lamentations 3:27.
[46] Ecclesiastes 3:1-8.

# CHAPTER TWELVE

# The Strong Man Versus the Angry Man

Son, what quality truly makes a man a man's man? What do you think you need to possess in order to be a real man? The typical answer to this question is different when asked in different cultures. Our culture more than anything else—including religion—dictates what we think a real man is. We get caught in stereotypes of what a man is and should be based on the culture in which we grow up.

For example, in the western culture of America, many people see the rugged, tough, gruff, hunter-type to be the epitome of what a man is. This man doesn't take flak from anyone. He can take a punch, and he rules his home with an iron fist of control. I've heard teachings on manhood where men are taught never to follow a woman and never do what a woman tells them to do—even if the advice is right, holy, and comes from a godly woman. This becomes the quality of a man's character in their eyes—that he doesn't listen to women.

Yet a man who believes such has either been taught wrong or is insecure in his manhood. In Proverbs, King Lemuel was given advice that a man in power and authority should not give his strength to women.[47] First, the warning is about women (plural), not about any specific woman (singular). Second, to every man reading this Scripture, you should know that the advice given to Lemuel came *from a woman*, specifically his mother. A woman said it. I've heard preachers use that verse to tell men not to listen to a woman, but by using the verse at all, these same men were following the advice of a woman. A secure man is not threatened at all by a strong woman. He can take advice from her. He can gain knowledge from her. He can pattern himself after her stronger character attributes. He can do this because he is secure in his manhood and in his role as a man. Insecure men need to always prove their dominance and exert control.

But a man isn't made by how much he can bench press, or by how many rounds he can go in a boxing match, or by how rugged he can be, or by how many deer he's shot, or by how well he plays sports. The one quality that makes a man a man's man is self-control.

The key to manhood is self-control.

The Bible is clear on this subject. We are told that a man who is "slow to anger is better than the mighty; and he that ruleth his spirit than he that taketh a city."[48] The second part of the verse is the key: he "ruleth his spirit." A man who can control himself is a man of power and strength. Of all things men control in life and on earth, controlling ourselves is the most difficult and requires the greatest discipline.

---

[47] Proverbs 31:3.
[48] Proverbs 16:32.

Another verse states, "He that hath no rule over his own spirit is like a city that is broken down, and without walls."[49] A man who cannot control himself, his emotions, and his actions is a weak, vulnerable man who can be controlled, conquered, and manipulated. A weak man can be controlled simply by manipulating his emotions. Since he has no self-rule, he is at the mercy of what others do to him. He explodes in anger when someone does something he doesn't like. He becomes mean-spirited toward those he thinks have treated him badly. He doesn't get angry on purpose or deliberately, but instead allows others to trigger his anger simply because he has no self-control.

Perhaps the greatest sign of a lack of self-control is how we use our tongue. When you get angry, the first sign of anger is typically the words that come out of your mouth. Your tongue is the ultimate expression of your manhood. Whatever controls your tongue controls your manhood. This is why the Bible says, "If any man offend not in word, the same is a perfect man, and able also to bridle the whole body."[50] A man who can control the tongue is a man who can control every other aspect of his character. He is disciplined. He is in control of his actions. He is able to act instead of reacting.

The search for self-control should probably start with the tongue, the words you say, how you say them, and when you say them. Also in this search should come something most men don't really find palatable: submission. When we think of submission, men in Christian circles typically think of women's submitting to men or a wife to her husband. But any power that is to be controlled must first be submitted, which is why God commands

---

[49] Proverbs 25:28.
[50] James 3:2.

a wife to submit to her husband because God knows the power she has over him. God wants that power to be controlled, and to control it properly, a wife must learn to submit. Otherwise, her power is out of control and will cause damage to the marriage and family. The same is true for a man. If we do not learn to submit ourselves to God, to others, and to holiness, we will never learn to control our power. And a sure sign of weakness is the destructiveness of power out of control.

The Bible teaches that being filled with God's Spirit requires submission: "But be filled with the Spirit...Submitting yourselves one to another in the fear of God."[51] Submission is also tied in with humility: "Wherefore he saith, God resisteth the proud, but giveth grace unto the humble. Submit yourselves therefore to God."[52] Pride is the bane of self-control, but humility is always evidence of self-control. Humility, however, doesn't happen without submission.

The two steps a man must take in order to gain self-control is, first, to learn to control his tongue, and that will never happen unless he, secondly, learns submission. These steps naturally lead into the realm of controlling one's temper. When a man loses his temper, he is neither controlling his tongue nor submitting. His anger rules all.

Even though anger itself is not a sin, and there are times when anger is absolutely the correct response, uncontrolled anger leads to a lack of self-control that is not okay.

The Bible gives two very direct warnings about an angry man. In the first, Solomon warns his son, "Make no friendship with an

---

[51] Ephesians 5:18-21.
[52] James 4:6-7.

angry man; and with a furious man thou shalt not go."[53] This verse is very direct. For many reasons, Solomon did not want his son to be friends with an angry man. An angry man will ultimately drag you into his problems. His lack of self-control means he will go places you do not want to go and do things you don't want to be associated with. But there is another reason. Friendship with an angry man means you will most likely become the target of his anger, especially when, as a friend, you try to correct him or prevent him from making a mistake.

Solomon then says the following about an angry man: "An angry man stirreth up strife, and a furious man aboundeth in transgression."[54] Keep in mind, son, that we are talking about someone who is easily angered and has no self-control. We're talking about someone who seems to be always angry. This person will stir up strife that would not normally exist. He will see insult where there is none. He will assume bad intentions when an accident occurs. He will imagine slight over the smallest things. A man like this will always be in trouble with the authorities in his life. This man will lead you into nothing but trouble.

Son, are you an angry man? Are you the man against whom Solomon was warning his son?

Learning to control your temper involves several things. Solomon explained to his son that a man "that is slow to wrath is of great understanding."[55] A person who can control his temper is a person who is able to see the other side of the equation. He can see things from someone else's perspective. If you get hit by a ball during a game, a man of understanding first looks to see if it was

---

[53] Proverbs 22:24.
[54] Proverbs 29:22.
[55] Proverbs 14:29.

an accident, but an angry man first assumes it was done on purpose. If someone doesn't shake your hand one day, a man of understanding looks to see if such a person is wrestling with a problem that lays heavy on their heart, but an angry man assumes the person has slighted and insulted him.

Learning to see things from someone else's perspective is a key to understanding. The key to seeing something from another point of view is to shut up and not say anything, but to listen. An angry person uses his mouth to express his anger, which is why James warns, "Wherefore, my beloved brethren, let every man be swift to hear, slow to speak, slow to wrath."[56] A progression can be seen in that verse:

1. If you are swift to hear...
2. Then you are slow to speak...
3. Which results in being slow to anger.

This progression doesn't mean that you should never get angry. What it does mean is that it should take quite a bit to get you angry. Anger should be focused and deliberate—not something that springs into being at the drop of a hat. Anger should never control you, son. You should always be in control of your anger.

The more you are able to see things from other points of view, the more your anger will be tempered, controlled, and properly directed. I'm always amazed at how easily people become angry over the smallest issues. Son, do not be that way. Learn to be in control of your anger. Learn to see things from someone else's perspective. The more you understand the situation and other people, the more you will know whether or not you should

---

[56] James 1:19.

get angry. Anger should be something that comes to you slowly, not quickly.

A real man is a man of understanding.

## Kill the Cat

Growing up, we had both dogs and cats. I remember the cats the most, however. In particular, we had an all-black cat except for a small patch of fur right under the chin who we named Sammy. Sammy grew to be a very large cat, weighing over fifteen pounds. To a young boy, I could have sworn he weighed over twenty. Sammy was very heavy, very large, and very strong.

Sammy possessed a peculiar personality of not liking people much, though he would protect children fiercely. But when he wanted to be petted, he would scratch you until you complied with his wishes. When he wanted you to stop, he'd scratch you again. He was so big that when I, at ten years old, carried him, his hind legs would dangle down past my knees, which made carrying him a bit dangerous. He also loved to pounce on you when you weren't looking.

While playing in our backyard one day, Sammy crawled up behind me and pounced. All of a sudden, a fifteen-pound fur ball crashed into my back, claws extended. I was standing near a small bench when I got hit, and the impact drove me right over the bench, sending me sprawling. Furious, I rolled over and saw Sammy watching me patiently from the grass a few feet away. I swear that cat wore such a smug expression that I simply lost my cool. I got so angry that the only thing I wanted to do was kill that stupid cat.

Our backyard on Lynn Lane in Phoenix had a pond that my dad had built. The pond was fairly large, looking like a squared 8 with a narrow channel that connected the upper and lower parts of the pond. My dad had built a bridge across that narrow neck and had stocked the four-foot-deep pond with fish and lilies. This seemed the perfect place to commit cat murder. Drowning a cat seemed poetic justice for a creature adverse to lots of water.

I tackled Sammy, who gleefully went about adding more stretches to the ones he'd already given me. I spun the cat over, yanked him off the ground, and lurched toward the pond. I had the idea that if I kept my back to the pond, Sammy would not know what I intended until it was too late. Just when I came in range, I spun around and let fly. Sammy soared out into the air, but that canny cat, spread out his claws, twisted in midair, and somehow managed to sink one set of claws into the palm of my left hand. What with his weight and my momentum, he tugged me right in after him.

We both hit the water with a tremendous splash. I got a mouthful of pond water as I gasped and floundered around in the lily pads, trying to make sense of what had just happened. I stood up, my anger shocked right out of me, and spit water. Sammy reached the edge first and pulled himself out. He shook himself, but instead of running away, he turned around and fixed a baleful glare at me.

I trudged toward the edge, but that stupid cat shifted position to meet me. I stopped, still standing in the pond as I realized Sammy fully intended to keep me in the water. This was still a game to that infernal feline! All that I had accomplished was getting myself soaked in a somewhat mossy pond and a bloody hand from the cat's claws. I splashed water at him until he got tired of dodging and wandered off, quite satisfied with himself no doubt.

My anger had accomplished nothing. Even if I'd succeeded in drowning that cat, I would have regretted it. I loved that cat, but my momentary anger had overwhelmed any other thought and feeling I had. And the stupid cat won. I had allowed a cat, of all things, to control me.

## A Sucker for Dirt

Growing up on the edge of Phoenix, I had a friend named Nick. Our families were friends, as Nick's uncle served as our pastor for quite some time. In fact, Nick's older sister used to babysit me as a kid—on one such babysitting session, I actually broke her arm during a wrestling match. Anyway, Nick and I did a lot of things together since he lived right down the street.

But being boys, we also argued and fought a lot. We were coming home from the nearby elementary school, Nevitt Elementary, and Nick had somehow gotten one of those huge, colorful suckers. To my first-grade eye, the sucker was gigantic, and I wanted some of it. I begged him for a piece, but he steadfastly refused. All the way home, I argued with him about it, growing more and more angry. I didn't see why he couldn't share. We were friends, and that sucker was ginormous! He wouldn't miss a little piece of it.

But he would just grin at me and deliberately lick the sucker. His refusal to share was infuriating! "Come on, Nick! Gimme a piece!"

"No!"

I shoved him. "You're mean!"

He shrugged, grinned, and licked again at the sucker.

I wanted to throw something at him, but nothing came readily to mind. It just wasn't fair.

And then some kid that I didn't know rode up on his bike. When he was perhaps eight feet away, he stopped, got off the bike, let it fall to the sidewalk, and walked up to the two of us. Without a word or even a hint, he reared back and punched Nick right in the mouth.

I jerked back startled and watched in a peculiar detachment as the sucker flew by my head and fell to the hot sidewalk, shattering. Nick reeled back, his hand going to his mouth and tears springing to his eyes. The other kid calmly, and still without saying a word, retrieved his bike and rode off.

I never did learn what that was all about, and to my shame, I only had one feeling: satisfaction. Now Nick wouldn't get the sucker either. In my little mind, I felt I'd somehow gotten a measure of revenge for his unwillingness to share. I didn't ask about the other kid. I didn't wonder if Nick was okay. I just felt satisfied that if I couldn't have any of the sucker, then neither could he.

That is what anger can do.

That wasn't the only time Nick and I got into it. My father had built a sandbox in the corner of our backyard. He had outlined the area with railroad crossties and then fetched a bunch of sand from the nearby Salt River. When the sand sat for a time or had been rained on, it grew somewhat hard and crusty. One of the things Nick and I loved to do was see how large of a dirt clod we could excavate from the sandbox. The bigger the better, naturally.

It became a competition. We would carefully dig out the loose sand and then lift the dirt clod up and into a wheelbarrow—

so that we could show them off, of course. Once we had gotten them into the wheelbarrow, we examined our treasures.

"I've got the biggest one," Nick announced happily.

I glumly realized his claim to be true. He did have the largest one. "Let's move them into the shade," I suggested, wiping my forehead. The Arizona sun was beating down on us. I picked up the wheelbarrow handle bars and rolled it into the shade next to the house, but the moment I set it down, Nick's dirt clod, the big one, split right in half.

He gasped. "You did that on purpose!" he yelled.

"Did not!" I protested just as loudly.

"Did too! He then brought his fist down on my dirt clod, smashing it flat.

I roared in anger and shoved him aside so I could stomp one of his other ones. We shoved, kicked, and threw awkward punches to get each other out of the way. The only thing we accomplished, however, was to demolish all the dirt clods, reducing them down to their individual grains of sand. We now had only a normal pile of regular sand in the wheelbarrow.

We yelled and screamed at each other, leveled accusations, and generally proclaimed our undying hatred of the other. When our anger played itself out, we naturally, as only little kids can do, became best friends again. But I did learn a lesson about anger. When you get angry, it can be over the dumbest things.

## "Shut Up, Darren!"

While in Bible college, I worked for a company called United Global Nippon (UGN). The company fabricated car parts for a variety of car manufactures, such as Honda, Nissan, and others. I worked on a Honda Civic process. We made a part that went into the dashboard designed to reduce engine noise from the cab. The part required a seven-man production team and involved a tar-rubber-like material that was glued to a piece of shaped and hardened fabric. We would then trim the piece and put clips around it so that it could be attached to the vehicle.

I was the only Christian working on the crew, and I was the only Bible-college student working in the molding department. I took some flak for it, but not too much. Until, that is, they conspired to get me angry. I'd not lost my temper before, though part of that was due to my fear of confrontation, so I typically held my peace and seethed internally rather than just letting someone have the full brunt of my anger. I rarely expressed my anger outwardly, but all six of the other guys on the crew got together and laid bets as to how long I could go without losing it.

So that Monday, things started to go wrong for me, obviously so, and obviously the men on my team were responsible. For example, when working with the barrier—the tar-rubbery sheet—we wore gloves because we had to heat up the barrier, toss it on to a press, and hit a control that sucked the pliable barrier down onto an ice-cold mold to shape it properly. Well, these crewmates of mine filled my gloves with glue so when I stuck my hand in it—well, you can no doubt image what happened.

They would hide things from me so that I'd get behind in my work, and then they would "bury" me while on the clipping position. The part we were making would be glued and then trimmed on a different press. The trimmed piece would be placed on a table for the clipper to snap seven clips into their designated spots. The clipper did not have an easy task. The clips required both hands to insert, and there was a trick to it that involved thumbs and twisting. The first time I had to do it, my hands hurt for days trying to keep up. So to further irritate me, the trimmer would toss trimmed pieces on the table faster than I could clip them. The pile got so high that I had to stand on the table to try to clip the topmost piece.

They laughed—and laughed even more when the finisher began yelling and cussing at me for being so slow. The harder I tried to catch up, the more they "buried" me so that when break time came, I used my entire break just catching up. My catching up didn't set well with the finisher who now had a large pile of his own to do once he came back from break. More yelling, more cussing, and more laughing took place.

The trimming press required pieces of Velcro on the edges to aid the cutting process because the press edges alone did not cut well. The co-conspirators hid the Velcro from me and then pretended they didn't know where it was, which forced me to struggle with the trimming. I often had to trim a piece two or three times before I could pass it on to the clipper. The clipper and finisher would yell and cuss at me for falling behind.

For five straight days, my coworkers continued to sabotage me, and all the time I grew angrier and angrier—on the inside. I began having vengeful thoughts, and even my supervisor laughed at me when I brought what they were doing to his attention. Then on Friday, I'd finally had enough. I could take their incessant pranks, ridicule, yelling, and cussing no more.

That day, Darren was finishing, and of all the men on the crew he was the most vocal, the most foul-mouthed of the whole lot. The rest knew this, and they knew that I didn't cuss and that I didn't like the cussing, so they purposely made me miserable and egged him on. Darren let loose with one of his profane rants at me, and I just snapped.

For me, snapping doesn't mean I fly into a rage. For me, losing control means doing what I would never do unless I absolutely had to. I forced a confrontation. I left my position and walked over to where Darren was doing the finish work.

"Darren," I said slowly and softly.

He paused and looked at me. "What?"

"Shut up."

I didn't yell it. I didn't scream. I didn't throw a punch. I didn't do anything but say those three words: "Darren, shut up." And then I dismissed him as if he were a pile of filthy trash with which I wanted nothing to do.

Darren was quite a bit larger than I. And for a long moment he just stood there with the rest of the crew watching on. I can only imagine all of them were astonished. I'd never done anything like that before, and until that moment, I'd just taken the punishment they had doled out to me all week. Once what I'd said sunk in, Darren came unglued. He left his position and ran after me, cussing and swearing at me and threatening all sorts of violence. I didn't care. I didn't care about him. I didn't care about the whole lot of them. I wished he'd throw a punch at me. All I needed was one little excuse, and I didn't care whether or not I'd get beaten up. For that moment, I lost all semblance of my Christianity, and I threw my testimony out the window.

Darren caught up to me and thrust himself in my way. I grunted, pushed him aside like he was so much deadweight and marched on. I was going to quit. I was going to march into my supervisor's office and tell him that I was quitting, that he could have the whole lot of worthless, idiots. I fully planned to give him an earful as well. I didn't care about the consequences. I just wanted to take whatever revenge I could get, and the best one I could think of was to quit, because in quitting, the rest of the crew would be a man down and they'd have weeks of rough going until someone could be properly trained to take my place. They deserved it. Every last one of them!

I was almost to the supervisor's door when two of the men from my crew intercepted me. "Whoa there, buddy," one of them said, a Mexican with long hair. "Where do you think you're going?"

"What's it to you?" I snapped. "Get out of my way."

The other, a solidly built man with a buzz haircut, held up his hand. "Greg, it's okay. We just had a bet about how long it would take you to lose your cool. Well, we know. We'll stop harassing you. Promise."

I froze, staring at them both in disbelief. This whole sabotage had been about a bet? All of this over my character? My first thought was to punch both of them in the mouth as hard as I could, but the second thought struck me much like when you foolishly walk into a wall you didn't even know was there, but everyone else did. I had a chance to allow my Christianity to shine, and I'd failed. Oh, I had lasted five days, but in truth, I really hadn't. Only my fear of confrontation had kept me from exploding sooner. Inside, I'd already lost control days before. I was reacting instead of acting. Instead of seeing the opportunity before me, I let them control and manipulate my emotions.

I had a good view of myself at that moment, and I didn't like what I saw. The last five days had been horrible, even when I wasn't at work because while I was away, I was still thinking about everything they were doing to me, and the situation had consumed so much of my thoughts that I had lost myself.

Well, I didn't quit. I didn't try to get revenge for what they'd done to me for those five days. I did ask them to forgive me—even asked Darren, who just grumbled something about staying out of his face—and went back to work. I felt humbled and embarrassed. Here I was to be a testimony of Jesus Christ, and despite lasting five days, I had no desire to show them Christ. Far from it. I'd actually had thoughts that they all deserved hell. I lost my cool. I lost control. And as soon as I did, all the rest of my Christianity disappeared as well.

Son, in what aspect of your character are you not in control? The moment you can no longer control yourself, you become weak.

# CHAPTER THIRTEEN
# When Things Go Wrong

Things will go wrong and things will break down. Accidents will happen. You will experience pain. Much of the trouble addressed in this book thus far comes from people. Because people are important, a man must learn to deal with people and all the problems inherent in any relationship. This chapter, however, will deal with the aspect of life that simply goes wrong, and there is no one really to blame or accuse—except for God.

I've met many people in life who blame God for what went wrong with their lives, things over which they had no control, things that just happened, and things that leave them in physical, emotional, and mental pain. These issues, however, are part of life, and they aren't fair. Why does one person get cancer and another doesn't? Why does a ladder break for one person and not another? Why does one person break an arm falling off a swing and another doesn't? Why does a healthy runner suffer a stroke when a lazy, overweight man doesn't? These questions—the "whys" of life—are often flung at God like ammunition.

A man must realize that life is life. Things are going to go wrong. They aren't your fault, and they aren't someone else's fault.

They aren't Satan's fault nor God's fault. We live in a sin-cursed world. The world is naturally entropic—tending toward chaos and disorder. Things get old and break down. Accidents happen.

Jesus spoke of this matter to His disciples when He asked them if the eighteen men killed by a falling tower in Siloam meant that God had targeted them because they were worse sinners than other men.[57] He said, "Nay: but, except ye repent, ye shall all likewise perish." In other words, unless we stay within God's sphere of protection, we can all fall victim to the randomness and chance that is this life.

Solomon, in his bitterness at the unexpected turns life had taken, observed that "the race is not to the swift, nor the battle to the strong, neither yet bread to the wise, nor yet riches to men of understanding, nor yet favour to men of skill; but time and chance happeneth to them all."[58] Outside of God's direct intervention, we are all at the mercy of life. Things happen.

Can God intervene? Absolutely. Does God allow things to go wrong in our life? Of course. Does that mean we can blame God for the things that go wrong? Nope. Blaming God for the things in life that go wrong is completely ridiculous. As Job discovered, where were you when God made the worlds? God sees the master plan—the end as well as the beginning. To blame God would be in effect to isolate yourself from the One who can intervene on your behalf. It is like blaming the fire department for not being at the site of a fire ahead of time to prevent a fire from starting. What purpose does it serve to become angry at the fire department because of a fire they didn't start? Worse, why would you cut

---

[57] Luke 13:4-5.
[58] Ecclesiastes 9:11.

yourself off from the very people who could help you get through the fire?

A man learns to roll with the punches of life. He doesn't cave in when things go wrong, and he learns to adapt to the situations God allows in his life. With the right attitude and understanding, any situation, no matter how negative, can be used for God's glory and your edification.

Life is filled with pain. Pain is not right or wrong; it just is. But the key is learning to heal from the wounds of life. Healing will invariably leave a scar, but a scar is simply a reminder of former pain. That scar doesn't hurt anymore. You can point to a scar and use it to help others or share your life with others.

However, wounds that aren't healed continue to throb and project pain. Even a slight brush against the wound will cause the pain to flare up, and you end up reliving it all over again. Being able to adapt and roll with the punches of life gives you the time and opportunity to heal. Remaining bitter, angry, and resentful is like constantly re-opening an old wound over and over again. It will never heal like that.

Stop blaming God or even life. Stop whining and complaining. This is the hand you've been dealt, so roll with it. That is what a real man does.

## Hammer in the Head

When I was, oh, six or seven years old, I had a friend who lived a couple houses down on at the end of our street whose name was Donnie. On one warm December afternoon—recall that I grew up in Arizona—I rode my bike over to his house. He was squatted down by the edge of the driveway and using a hammer to attack with gusto some object hidden from my immediate view.

Being naturally curious, I moved over to take a look. As I neared, I couldn't see anything, just dirt. Still curious, I stepped closer and bent over to get a better look when Donnie decided to give the object of his attention a really good smack. He hauled back to slam the hammer into the ground as hard as he could, not even realizing I'd slipped up behind him. Instead, the claw end of the hammer hit me right above my left eye.

The blow knocked me back several steps. For a moment, I stood there, feeling unsure. That's when I noticed the hammer was dangling from my head. I reacted by jerking it out. Immediately, blood gushed over my eye and down my face.

I was hurt, and I knew it. But what to do? Dad had taught me not to leave my things laying around—particularly at my friends' houses. So, despite the fact that pain filled my head like someone had unleashed the full fury of a major hailstorm right inside my skull, I just couldn't leave my bike lying on the sidewalk.

So I climbed up on the bike, crying in pain, and rode the three houses down to my house. I weaved the whole way there, trying to hold the blood back with one hand and riding with only one eye. I left a trail of blood from Donnie's house to my house, but I got the bike home. That I did. I ran inside imploring help from my mother who was decorating the Christmas tree we'd set up in the living room. She took one look at me and all the blood on my face and sighed. Boys. She had two of them, and nearly all my cousins were boys, so my bloody face certainly didn't surprise her much.

The hole in my head healed, but left a scar right above and to the side of my left eye. I had come within a quarter of an inch of losing my eye. The injury hurt, as you no doubt know, but it also healed. Every time I see that scar, I remember what happened. Trust me, I am a bit more cautious around people who are swinging hammers.

Did Donnie mean to hit me? Of course not. He didn't even know I was there. Does that mean we should ban all children from ever swinging a hammer? Let's not get crazy. There is no way to avoid every situation that can go wrong. It was merely an accident. But what if I'd lost an eye? No matter what we could have done after that—sue Donnie's family, rage at the night sky at the unfairness of it all, or curse God—it would not have changed what happened. I would have had to learn to live with it. That's all.

## The Same and the Opposite

A girl attended Bible college with me who had been born with some disease that left her a cripple for life. She was wheelchair bound, had her arms in slings, had a frail body, and bore a hunchback that protruded sharply just below her neck. She would never get married, have children, or live the life that most of us hope to have. Until God took her to heaven, she would always be at the mercy of her caregivers.

But what a spirit she had! She laughed all the time, teased everyone uncomfortable around her crippled body, and made jokes about her crippled state that put everyone to shame. She had such an amazing ability, at least in public, to just enjoy the life she had. She was dependent upon everyone for practically every aspect of her life. To get her into chapel, four men would have to carry her in her wheelchair down the steps, and she would make comments on the size of their muscles while they did it! She had a mischievousness about her that just made it fun to be around her.

At this time, I was preaching in the jails. My assigned spot was Division 8, the hospital division of Cook County Jail. This was where anyone who was injured or who required medical treatment was assigned. On one Sunday, I walked into the various rooms to invite the inmates to my service to be held in the rec room. In one room, I met a wheelchair-bound man and was immediately struck with the similarities between his condition and the girl in college.

He too was wheelchair-bound and would never be able to walk. His arms were in slings as well, and he too had a thin, emaciated body with an obvious protruding hunch in his back. Like the girl in college, he would never get married, never have children of his own, and was dependent upon others for nearly every aspect of his life.

I walked up to him and offered my hand. "Hi. I'm Greg. I run a church service in the rec room, and I wanted to invite you to come."

He gave me the coldest scowl I think I've ever gotten from a person. He cursed me, spit at my feet, and said, "If there's a God, He's evil. No loving God would have allowed me to be created like this!" He spat again and used the little joystick on his wheelchair to back away from me. He bumped into the wall, cursed, and tried to turn to put me at his back. He then swore at me again and ordered me out of the room.

I stared at him. My attempts to be friendly had been rebuffed so curtly, so thoroughly that I'm not sure I'd ever before experienced such absolute and dogmatic rejection. His bitterness exuded from every pore in his body. He absolutely hated life. He hated the way he was. He hated God for making him that way. He hated anyone who so much as even tried to be friendly to him. From his perspective, friendliness was simply a cover for pity.

He was in jail, so of a certain he had done something to earn his incarceration. I had no doubt his anger and bitterness were at the root of whatever he had done. He was such a contrast to that girl in school.

One was happy, the other miserable. One loved life, the other hated it. One could laugh easily, the other cursed and spit easily. They were in nearly identical physical conditions, but they could not have been more opposites of each other. Neither was responsible for how they were born. The only person they could blame was God. One chose to turn to God and found joy even in her situation. The other blamed God and led a miserable existence in his own head as well as in body.

The girl had more courage and strength than the man did. He couldn't adapt. He couldn't accept his situation. He couldn't move on and use his state to find a way to enjoy life. In his eyes, God had failed him even as his body had failed him, but in doing so, he became as crippled in his spirit as he was in body. He robbed himself of so much joy.

## Making the Most of a Bad Situation

Our church youth group left to go on a camping trip one Friday morning during the summer. I was perhaps fifteen at the time, and our youth leader, Dean, wanted the trip to be a bonding time with the teenagers. We'd been going through youth pastors like one goes through old clothes to throw away. Men would come, stay a while, and then depart, leaving behind a bit of bitterness and rebellion in the hearts of the teenagers. Dean was a layman in the church, and he volunteered to work with the teenagers until another youth pastor could be found.

We weren't a bad group of kids, just jaded from a seemingly long line of bad choices in the men who had claimed they loved us, but from our eyes, did not. So we, as a group, didn't really trust outsiders, but Dean wasn't an outsider. He'd been part of the church for years. He was a big man with a beard and an analytical mind. I took to him easily enough for I liked his mindset. The other teenagers tolerated him because he had stepped up when no one else had.

This camping trip was meant to help revive the spirit of the teenagers, and so a great deal of prayer and planning had gone into it. We were to rough it, sleeping overnight in tents. We had two men and two women chaperons on the trip, and everything had been cared for to ensure that gender boundaries would not be crossed. Our goal was a place above Payson, Arizona, in the forested mountains near the East Verde River. Activities had been planned. Prayer had been offered. And a lot of parents were hoping that this activity would really make a difference.

My brother, Kevin and I, were on the trip along with perhaps twenty other teenagers. Because of the number of teens and chaperons, we took one of the church buses.

That's when it all went wrong.

The bus broke down near Lion Canyon about 20 miles south of Payson. Breaking down in the Arizona desert, sixty miles away from any church help in a time and era where cell phones had yet to be invented, and with the temperature peaking at nearly 110° is perhaps not the best of situations. To get help, one of the adults would need to hitch a ride into a town, find a phone, make some phone calls, organize help, and then hitch a ride back to the stranded teenagers, wait for help to arrive, and pray that we could get the bus fixed enough to limp back into Mesa, Arizona. This was going to take time—a lot of time.

Blaming God for this breakdown would have been easy. We could just as easily have blamed Satan. But the odds are that neither was directly responsible. Sometimes, things break down. We live in a sin-cursed world, and as a result, things just go bad. We can rant, rave, or blame whoever we want, but griping just doesn't change things. Did this mean that all the prayer that went into the trip was for nothing? Does this mean God didn't care? Does this mean Satan saw an opportunity to ruin God's plans? In all likelihood, the bus just broke down all on its own, and no one was to blame unless you wanted to blame Adam and Eve for eating of the forbidden fruit.

But now a reality existed that was what it was. God can take any situation and turn it to His glory and purpose. Satan would love to do the same thing for his purpose, and this is where the real battle is. Things going right or wrong does not necessarily determine who won the battle. It is what we do with the situation we find ourselves in. What do we take away from it? Can we take a bad situation and turn into something good?

Here we were, twenty hot teenagers stranded in the middle of nowhere, with all our plans gone completely awry. So what do we do? Hey, we were teenagers. What do you think we did? We found a way to enjoy the situation.

To get us to expend our pent-up energy, Dean suggested we climb to the top of a peak directly east of where the bus had broken down. He offered a prize to the first one to make it to the top. The prospect of winning a prize sent nearly the entire group of teenagers barging down the slope of the ravine and then clambering up the other side to reach the top.

My brother and I had spent more time trudging around the desert and mountains than the rest of the teenagers, so I took a moment to scope out the best way up the peak. If you went straight down and then straight up, you'd be forced to climb a sharp slope at the end that looked a bit daunting. However, off to the side of the peak, a finger of the mountain jutted out toward us at much more amicable slope. If we went up that way, we would end up to the south of the peak, but at an angle that would allow us to climb to the top much more easily than the route the rest of the teenagers were taking—the direct, straight-up approach.

"Kevin," I said, holding my brother back as the other teenagers took off. "Not that way. Follow me."

Jimmy, another of the teenagers, hesitated when he heard that. He took one look at us and declared, "I'm going with you."

Instead of running straight down and then straight up, we went south, found the gentler slope, and ran up to the crest and then back north to the top of the peak. We beat the rest of the teenagers easily and were waiting there, feet dangling off a large rock, when the first of the teenage guys, huffing and puffing from exertion, pulled himself up to the crest.

He took one look at us, and his face soured. "How'd you get there so fast?" he demanded.

I gave him an innocent look. "We just walked here," I said trying to sound casual.

He snorted. "Yeah, right. No. Really. How'd you get up here so fast?"

"We took a shortcut."

He blinked. He had taken the most direct route. Any other route would be longer distance wise, but not necessarily in time or effort. Sometimes, the shortest distance between two points is not a straight line. I imagine God sometimes does this in our lives. In trying to build our character and lives, He may take us on a circular route that may seem like a detour but is, in reality, the quickest way to where He wants us to be.

When we came down off the mountain, we discovered a large galvanized culvert into which we could walk. This culvert ran under the highway and handled rain runoff for those times when we actually got rain. This one still had a bit of standing water in it, but what really made it intriguing to us teenagers was the fact that it went in for about twenty yards and then angled up about twelve feet before running another twenty yards straight to the other side of the highway.

The highway at this location was divided with a twenty-yard median between the roads. The southbound lanes were about twenty feet higher up, however, leaving a gully or trench in the median. The culvert went under the northbound lanes, up twelve feet, and then under the southbound lanes, exiting out near a gully that caught rainwater from the western slope of some large mountains.

And inside…there were bats. At least one flew out, startled by our presence.

We had found the perfect situation for teenagers to show their mettle and daring. We stood at the entrance to the culvert for a time, peering in, and daring each other to climb to the other side. Group mentality is a strange phenomenon. What each of us would not have dared to do on our own—particularly with bats inside, and yes, we were all thinking of vampire bats—we decided to do as a group. We went in, bats and all. We didn't know if vampire bats were native to Arizona or not, but that possibility didn't stop us from assuming they were, so we were feeling pretty brave.

About ten of us braved the culvert. The rest decided to see if we'd survive. After all, who knew what lay at the top of the culvert?

We went in to where the culvert angled up at a slightly greater than a 45°angle. The ridged culvert was slick and dark, and making it up to the top looked to be a challenge. Several of us tried to climb up, but ended up sliding back down as the water had created a slick slide of sorts. We talked it over and then decided to send my brother up next. Kevin, like me, was thin and skinny, long legged, wiry and agile. He spread himself wide, trying to find stable hand

and footholds while trying to avoid the slick parts. He spider-walked slowly to the top.

When he got up there, he shouted down, "There's light. I can see the other side." There was a pause. "There's another bat up here!"

"You next, Greg," one of the other boys said. "When you get to the top, you can help pull me up."

The plan sounded like a decent one. "Okay," I replied. I examined the ridged culvert. If my brother could make it up, then so could I. A firm rule put in place for all older siblings is never to let your younger brother show you up. I could not allow this rule to be broken now. I started up.

My tennis shoes, scrambled for footing on the slick surface, and I had to use my fingers in the ridges to keep myself from tumbling back down, but like Kevin, I managed to spider-walk to the top. I hauled myself over and found my brother standing just at the top, a bright-white spot from the exit making him more of a dark, formless shadow. "Hi Greg," he offered, seeing me pull myself up.

I grunted in response, thinking sarcastically, *He's been a big help.* I turned around, laid down off to one side where the culvert wasn't that wet, and stuck my hand over the side. "I'm up," I called down. "Come on."

The next teenage boy to make the attempt was a stocky, heavy-set fellow a few years older than I. Twelve feet is a long way up, and his approach to get to the top was novel, if anything. He backed up, took a running start, and tried to run up the angled culvert. His first step was off to the side of the slick area where he got some decent traction. He took one more step up, and then lunged for my outstretched hand.

I grabbed his hand just as it came in reach. "Got you!"

That's when the full weight of his greater mass pulled at my arm. With a yell from the two of us, he pulled me right over, and we both went sliding down twelve feet to the bottom—him feet first and me face first. We crashed together in a jumble of arms, legs, and wet sand.

Someone laughed, though I didn't really think it to be a laughing matter. I slowly got to my feet and peered up at the top where my brother was poking his head over. "You okay?" he asked.

"Yeah," I replied, refusing to admit to any number of scrapes and bruises. "Let's try that again."

We did try, but only one other boy made it up the slick culvert to join Kevin at the top. I tried several more times, but by that time, my shoes and hands were wet, and I couldn't get any traction at all. Kevin and the other teen boy inched their way out the other side of the culvert on their own, fending off a solitary bat that didn't want to leave the dark culvert. We laughed, teased, and joked about my fall down the culvert. As a group, we were bonding. By struggling together, we had become much closer. This bonding included me, an introverted loner who really wasn't fond of my own peer group.

Not far from where our bus broke down, we heard movement in the twenty-yard-wide median between the divided highway. We went over to investigate and found an injured javelina, a large rodent that looked somewhat like a pig and roamed the Arizona desert. The "j" is pronounced with an "h." This nearly 40-pound javelina had been hit by a car and had a broken spine. The animal could not move its hind legs, so it was going to die. None of us, except perhaps me, had ever been this close to a javelina, and so we were fascinated by the creature.

Someone suggested, "We need to put it out of its misery."

That suggestion sparked a debate, where some, mostly the girls, were in favor of not killing it and just leaving it alone, but the fact that the animal was going to die anyway became quickly obvious. The javelina was crazy with fear and pain, snapping at us, but unable to flee or even inch away. We elected to kill it, ending its misery.

This decision presented a problem. None of us—not even the adults—had a weapon outside of a pocketknife. As brave as we were, none of us wanted to jump the creature and stab it over and over with a small pocketknife to end its misery. So we hunted around for something that would work. Eventually we found an old signpost—the kind made out of metal that had two edges and a concaved center where the sign would've actually been attached. We worked it out of the ground, and with our homemade "javelina killer," we proceeded to bash the poor thing on the head as hard as we could.

This attempt to dispatch the animal did not go quite according to plan. Not only did the javelina have a hard skull, our weapon of choice simply didn't have the right weight or mass distribution to make a great club that could easily put down the creature. One of the older teenage boys got elected to have the honors of bashing the animal. He took his stance and swung mightily. He hit the head, but the angle simply caused the post to slide off. The javelina barked, snapped even more furiously, and glared at us like it wanted nothing more than to return the favor.

We made quite a sight. Twenty teenagers standing between a divided highway while one of them swung a signpost at a helpless, injured animal. I can only imagine what passing motorists must have thought upon seeing us.

Several of us had a go at it, and I'm telling you, ending that animal's misery probably took something like fifty blows. By the time we finished, all of us were feeling a little sick. What should've been a quick death ended up being a torturous, bloody, and painful ending. We gathered around the carcass somewhat solemnly, though one or two did try to make a joke in an effort to deflect the uncomfortable moment.

Death had found us on that lonely stretch of desert—death we'd dealt out ourselves for a seemingly good cause. As a group, we bonded in ways we'd never had before. I suspect that if we'd safely gotten to our destination and not have gone through this particular struggle, we'd have never grown as close as we did. Many of the teenagers took away some valuable lessons from the experience, including me. I don't think I'd have nearly the strong memories I do if we'd actually gone on the camping trip. Being stranded, going through some hardship served our youth group much better.

We all came away from it different. Even though I don't personally believe we could blame the bus breaking down on God or Satan, God used the situation to His glory. It was what it was. But we got a lot more out of something going wrong than we probably would have if everything had gone according to plan.

We'd fallen victim to Murphy's Law, but that doesn't mean we had to be a victim or act like victims. We made the most out of a bad situation and came out much better for the experience.

Son, what situation in your life has not gone according to plan? What are you going to take away from it?

# CHAPTER FOURTEEN
## Step Up, Son

So many qualities are important to manhood. This one, I believe, is essential. Son, there will be times when you need to step up to the plate, where every eye is on you, where everyone is counting on you, and where the result may hinge on what you do. This position is not a comfortable one to be in, but God always calls upon a man to step up and be counted.

Men don't flee from situations where they are called upon to step up; they embrace them. That doesn't mean you won't be scared. That doesn't mean you won't fear failing. And it doesn't mean you won't actually fail. You very well might. But in truth, I'd rather have a man who steps up and fails than a man who runs away because he fears failure.

Our natural protective tendencies don't want us to get involved in something that we might fail at doing. No one likes to disappoint others. No one likes to look bad in front of others. No one wants to feel like a failure. Because of this fear of failure, we naturally resist stepping up in those areas where we lack confidence. Sometimes, however, we must step outside of our comfort zone and get the job done that needs doing.

Moses is a great example of someone stepping up despite his fears. Not only did Moses adamantly believe he was the wrong person for the job, he tried repeatedly to get out of doing it. When God called to him from the burning bush and explained what He wanted Moses to do, Moses resisted strenuously.[59] He first made the case that he was not the right man for the job and that someone else would be better. When that excuse failed, he tried to convince God that people would not naturally believe that he, Moses, could represent God. His next attempt was an effort to convince God that the Israelites would not believe him, so there was no point in going. When that pretext failed, he tried to convince God that he didn't have the right skillset or ability to do the job.

In each case, God provided a means to overcome Moses' objection. All God needed Moses to do was to step up. God would take care of the rest. At first, Moses was content to remain in the background and let his older brother, Aaron, do all the talking. However, before long Moses stepped up and did the job that needed doing. His task wasn't easy. At first, he seemed to be a complete failure, but little by little, he gained the confidence he needed from God to see the task through.

Son, I'd not give two cents worth for a man who is unwilling to step up when he's needed. There will be times when your parents need you, your family needs you, your wife needs you, your friends need you, your followers need you, your church needs you, and your God needs you. You need to step up. It shouldn't matter if the job is difficult. It shouldn't matter if you might fail. Sometimes, all God is looking for is for someone to step up.

---

[59] Exodus 3:10-14; Exodus 4:1-17.

Learn to take on responsibility. Learn to recognize need. And then step up if there is no one else able or willing to do so. As a child or teenager, son, you can step up. There are plenty of places in your family and church where you can step up. The job may be nerve-racking. The job may mean you have to make sacrifices. The job may mean all eyes will be on you. The job may mean no one will notice if you do it right—only if you do it wrong. It doesn't matter. Step up, son, and be counted.

## "What a Jerk!"

During my years in Bible college, I was given leadership of the Overcomers Bible Club, a college-run ministry that ministered to public school teenagers in the city area of Highland. On Sundays, the B-3 bus route, also a ministry of the Bible Clubs, would pick up the teenagers and take them to church.

For whatever reason, I became the club leader of a bunch of college goofballs who worked with me to reach teenagers. Honestly, I felt like I was watching a rolling comedy show every Saturday and Sunday. Two of these guys, Dustin and Jack, had this little act they put on with a plastic baseball bat. We often met in parking lots after Saturday visitation to discuss results and make plans for Sunday. These two would take my plastic baseball bat and proceed to pretend to beat the tar out of each other. They were good…very good. It looked very real.

They'd pretend to knock each other across the hood of cars, smash each other into the ground, and slam each other against walls. Jack was the bigger of the two, and I think Dustin often got the short end of the stick as far as acting like he was the one being beaten up, but they certainly enjoyed their harmless pastime until, that is, the police were called on us.

Here I am the leader of this motley group of college kids who were pretending to beat the fire out of each other with this real-looking, but entirely plastic, baseball bat when a police car came rolling up. The officer rolled down his window and yelled, "What are you guys doing?"

You must understand. We didn't exactly *look* like a bunch of rambunctious gangbangers. We all wore dress clothes and ties. So, yeah, two guys in ties and buttoned-up dress shirts looked sort of odd to be beating each other up. Probably, their appearance was the only thing that saved Dustin and Jack from being arrested right then and there.

I stepped over. "They're just goofing off, officer. The bat is plastic, and they're just faking it."

He considered my words. "I see. Well someone called that there was a fight in the parking lot, so please be careful."

He drove off and left us laughing that Dustin and Jack had been so convincing the police had been called on them.

This happened twice more. The next instant didn't involve the police—just a group of guys in a truck who drove up while Dustin and Jack were doing their "thing." When we explained what was happening, they drove off, somewhat huffy as I recall. On the last occasion, the police showed up again, but this time they wanted our names and birthdays.

Dale, one of the guys with us, asked, "Are you going to send us a birthday card?" The officer gave Dale such a cold look that Dale held up his hands and backed away, a sloppy grin spread across his face. "Sorry," he said. "Just asking."

"We need this in case the police are called on you guys again," the officer replied.

Well, that answer gave Dustin and Jack an idea. Once or twice a semester, the pastor of our church gave the college girls permission to ride the night bus after the Sunday evening service. The night bus was typically more rambunctious than the bus routes in the morning. At night, we picked up the more diehard church attenders, so the college students typically let their hair down, so to speak, on the night bus. We'd preach at each other, we'd laugh, goof off, and just generally have more fun. The college girls were not usually allowed to ride the night bus for a number of reasons, but mostly because of safety issues. But our pastor had recently granted the girls permission to ride the night bus for the upcoming Sunday.

Everyone at the college had already heard about how the police and been called on Dustin and Jack for their antics with my plastic baseball bat. So these two goofballs came to me and begged to throw some sort of night bus show for the teenagers and the college girls who would be riding (which included their girlfriends). They wanted to stage a fight between them and get the teenagers to pick sides and cheer them on, but to actually have someone call the police and really get them arrested.

"Are you serious?" I demanded, having visions of everything going terribly wrong. My instinct was to squash this idea completely before it got out of hand. I just wasn't the daring type, and I could envision a million ways this fun could go bad.

"Yes," Dustin said excitedly. "It'll be great! We've got it all planned out." They told me the plan.

"You're nuts," I said. "There's no way that is going to work the way you want it to. The police are liable to keep you in jail just to punish you for annoying them."

Both Dustin and Jack looked crestfallen. Fulfilling this plan was important to them. They'd put a lot of thought into it, and they were asking me, as their leader, to step up and help. I knew instinctively that their idea was a profound mistake. I couldn't responsibly sanction such an action; besides, the whole thing went way outside my comfort zone. Still, if I didn't step up, they'd most likely try something anyway.

I reconsidered. I could see how this idea could be a great promotion to get riders to come to church. We could really hype it up. The teens would come just to see Dustin and Jack fight—after all, everyone had heard about the police showing up before. As a side note, seeing the look on everyone's face when the police hauled away Dustin and Jack would certainly be fun, but their plan needed revision. This meant I'd need to get involved.

"Okay, guys, there is only one way we can do this. Saturday, we'll drop by the Griffith Police Department and see if we can't get one of the officers to come by at a certain time and place and arrest you. But we've got to give them a reason to do it beyond an actual fight which will get you actually arrested. So we'll make it educational. After the stunt, we'll have the officer come on the bus and talk to us about real police procedures, and we'll allow the teens to ask questions."

They were all for the idea. The educational part, admittedly, was merely the "reason" for staging the stunt to get the two guys arrested. But by stepping up as I did, however, I was taking full responsibility for the outcome—good or bad. So if we were going to do it, it needed to be done in a way that wouldn't land me in jail or expelled from college either.

That Saturday, Dustin, Jack, Payne (the night bus captain), and I went to the Griffith Police Department. We laid out the plan, and I made sure to stress the educational part of it. The Chief of Police was there with one of his men, Sergeant Tully. They listened noncommittedly at first. When I finished explaining what I wanted, the Chief of Police turned to Sergeant Tully. "What do you think?" he asked.

Tully shrugged. "I'll do it."

The Chief of Police looked back at our bright and happy faces. "But only if we don't have an emergency or a call that we must deal with at the time. If a call comes in, we won't show up."

We agreed, seeing the sense of that and began praying that crime would take a vacation on Sunday night.

The next evening, we pulled the night bus into an empty strip mall parking lot at the edge of the small town of Griffith, Indiana. We told everyone to stay on the bus. Dustin and Jack, dressed in costumes (kinda like professional wrestling, except much more modest) began their play fight in the parking lot.

I stood outside with Payne, wondering if the police were going to show up. Dustin and Jack ranged all over, beating each other senseless—apparently—to the cheers and advice of the watching teenagers and college students on the bus.

"They've been going at it for a while," Payne said, looking off into the darkness. "I don't think he's coming."

I sighed. "That's a bummer. Let's give him a little more time. If not, we'll call it."

Dustin and Jack continued to fight, but obviously they were wearing down, and all of us who were in the "know" were growing disappointed that the police hadn't showed up. But then Sergeant Tully did show up. Without any warning, the lights of a police car appeared out of nowhere, accompanied with the high pitched siren.

Sergeant Tully slammed to a stop just in front of Dustin and Jack and shot out of his police cruiser. "What's going on here?" he demanded, stalking over to the fighters. He grabbed them both by the scruff of their necks and literally slammed them down onto the hood of the cruiser. I cringed. That actually sounded like it hurt.

I started to walk forward. I had told Tully to be belligerent, that we would try to explain what was going on, but for him to just get mad and haul off our two guys. I said, "We're a church group, officer. They weren't really fighting. They were just acting."

"A church group!" he roared. "This!" He stabbed a finger at Dustin and Jack. "This is a church activity? What sort of church are you from?"

I cringed. That actually seemed like a legitimate criticism based on what we were doing. Promoting a fight? Even a fake one? I opened my mouth to explain further, but he jerked Dustin and Jack up from the hood and handcuffed them to each other.

"If you want these guys, you can come down to the station and bail them out." He then shoved Dustin and Jack in the back of his cruiser, jumped in the front seat, slammed the door, and drove off.

You could hear a pin drop on the bus. Everyone just stared in absolute shock. No one could believe it. Yes, it really was funny to those of us in the know. Finally, one girl broke the silence by saying, "What a jerk!"

As if that phrase ignited a fire, everyone began shouting and talking. One girl, one of the girlfriends of the now-arrested actors, started to cry. Meanwhile, Payne and I were stalling as we slowly climbed back onto the bus. "Did you see which police force he was from?" I asked, loud enough for everyone to hear. Since we were right there on the edge of two municipalities, it would be a tossup as to which one it could have been.

"No," Payne answered, playing along. "It could have been Highland."

We discussed it for a bit longer when one of the teenagers shouted, "Look! They've escaped!"

We all spun around to see Dustin and Jack, still handcuffed together, come running frantically back toward the bus. Sergeant Tully had just driven them around the corner of a building and let them out. No one knew that, however, and it looked like they'd somehow managed to escape.

Behind them, lights flaring and siren blaring, came Sergeant Tully's police cruiser in hot pursuit. Just before reaching us, the police car slammed to a stop and Tully jumped out and chased Dustin and Jack on to the bus.

You've never seen such chaos. Teens and college girls were screaming and trying to get out of the way as Dustin and Jack tried to shove their way toward the back of the bus. When Sergeant Tully leaped up the stairs and into the bus, people became even more frantic, convinced that there would be a fight right there in the middle of the bus.

That was my cue to settle everyone down. I did, explaining what we'd done and that now we wanted to hear from Tully as to what he would've actually done in a real situation like this. This was the educational part I had inserted into the plan to give it some symbolism of legitimacy.

There was only one thing I hadn't done. I hadn't gotten permission to do any of this from the ministry leader to whom I answered. I'd stepped up all right, but I hadn't completely done so. Despite the fact that I'd mitigated the rather foolish plan and changed it into something with at least the facade of reason, I still should have gotten the whole plan cleared with Bro. Winter first.

In that respect, I had failed in my responsibility. My decision not to talk to Bro. Winter first showed how I truly felt. I believed

Bro. Winter would not have granted us permission to do what we wanted to do. So I determined that asking for forgiveness was easier than asking for permission. This is a coward's play—a refusal to step up to the plate when I should have. Dustin and Jack at least had brought the idea to me, their Bible Club leader, instead of simply going out and doing it on their own. I didn't give my leader, Dr. Winter, the same courtesy.

I did have enough character to decide that I'd talk to Bro. Winter first thing Monday morning. I didn't want him to find out from someone else and then call me into his office. I could at least step up to explain what I had allowed. I figured it would be better to take the bull by the horns, so to speak, and come clean right off.

So Monday morning, I went in search of Bro. Winter. By the time I had found him, he had already heard the story from two or three other people. Apparently, the story had gotten around to the entire college that previous night. Everyone knew about it—including Bro. Winter.

When I approached him, I said, "Bro. Winter, I need to tell you what happened last night—"

He held up a hand to stop me. "Greg, I already know." He gave me a rather chilly look. "You should have come and told me about this beforehand." Then, not giving me a chance to say anything in my defense, he simply walked away, leaving me standing alone and quite chagrinned in the middle of the hallway.

I needed to step up for Dustin and Jack, and I did. But I also needed to step up and meet my responsibilities as a Bible Club Leader. In that last, I failed. Son, you will have many times in your life where you will need to step up. Fear, anger, insecurity, and even selfishness can get in the way of your stepping up.

## Step Up to the Plate

Sometimes, the hardest things to do in life is to step up to do something that you already failed at, got hurt at, or was mocked for. Something of this nature happened to me in the seventh grade. That year, I was a skinny kid with shiny braces. During our physical education class, the teacher decided that we needed to play some softball. That decision was fine with me. I liked baseball. How hard could softball be?

When my turn came to bat, I stepped up to the plate to hit. Strangely, I bat and golf left-handed despite the fact that I am right-handed in everything else. My left-handedness in batting has to do with the way my dad, whose arms could only hold and swing the bat left-handed, had taught me. Both my brother Kevin and I bat this way. I got up to bat and hit a solid grounder toward the shortstop. I spun and dashed with blazing speed toward first base.

The shortstop, I remember, was a true left-hander. He fielded the ball, pivoted to line himself up, and launched the ball as hard as he could toward first base. His aim was off by a lot. The ball caught me squarely in the mouth in midstride. The impact was such that it literally knocked me out cold. Witnesses told me later that it looked like I'd just collapsed straight down to the ground. I don't remember any of what happened.

I do remember coming to a bit later and seeing a crowd of people bending over me. "Greg, are you okay?" someone stupidly asked.

I attempted to mumble something, but I began choking on all the blood in my mouth. When the softball had hit me, my braces had shredded the inside of my mouth like a cheese grater. Trust me, that hurt! My mouth quickly puffed up like a swollen balloon and turned all sorts of interesting colors. I could hardly talk or eat. To say the least, eating was a study in pain management.

About two weeks later, our teacher sent us all back out to the baseball field for more softball. When my turn to bat came up, I felt a particular chill go down my spine. I didn't want to step up to the plate again. My last experience hadn't gone so well.

"Step up to the plate," the teacher told me. "It's your turn, Greg."

"I'm good," I told him. "I don't need to bat."

I could tell he understood the source of my hesitation, so I hoped he would show me some mercy. He didn't. "You need to get back in there," he pointed out. "Go on. Step up to the plate."

My mind imagined all sorts of things that could go wrong. I still hesitated.

"You need to do this, Greg."

*Fine.* Grimacing, I stepped up to the plate and prepared to bat. Honestly, since this was slow pitch softball, I wasn't afraid that the pitcher would hit me. I was more afraid that I'd get hit when I wasn't looking during my run to first base again. For the first few pitches, I didn't swing. I was content with striking out.

My team, however, began muttering. I could hear the players talking. For a moment there, I just didn't care. *Let them talk.* I didn't want to get hit in the mouth by the ball again. But then something inside of me rose up to the occasion. *They're counting on me.* We had a man on third, and we were down by one run. *They need me.* It was a little thing, but it was enough. I hit the next pitch, a hard ground ball—right to the shortstop again. I took off running, but a fear rose up inside of me when I realized I was in the exact same situation as when I got hurt.

I could stop which would have probably prevented my being hit again, and in truth, that is exactly what I wanted to do. Or, I reasoned, I could run harder and beat the throw. I opted for choice two and took off. I will admit, however, that I raised my left hand in front of my face right as I was approaching the bag. I didn't get hit and I didn't get out, but I was still sweating. The thrown ball was still awfully close.

I stepped up. Will you, son?

# CHAPTER FIFTEEN
# Pride's Folly

All sin can be traced back to pride. The original sin harbored in the heart of Satan long before Eve ate of the tree of the knowledge of good and evil was pride.[60] Every other sin starts with pride. In fact, all sin can be categorized into three types, all of which are forms of pride:

1. The lust of the flesh
2. The lust of the eyes
3. The pride of life[61]

The Bible teaches us that all contention with other people is a result of pride.[62] So, son, when you get in a fight with your parents or one of your brothers or sisters, then you have pride in your heart. If you had no pride and even if they did have some, then there would still be no fight. Pride is perhaps your greatest challenge in life. Of all things to conquer, conquering your pride will be the hardest and will be the battle you fight most often. If

---

[60] Isaiah 14:12-15.
[61] 1 John 2:16.
[62] Proverbs 13:10.

you search your motivations for everything you do, you will most likely find elements of pride that factored into your decisions.

Pride and ego are closely related. Ego, in essence, is your self-image—how you see yourself and how you want other people to see you. If that image is harmed either through your own actions, such as embarrassment or through someone else's words, then your pride will rush to the rescue in an attempt to preserve or repair that image.

Son, your pride is the single greatest reason why you get into trouble. You will fight tooth and toenail to preserve your ego and maintain a particular image both in your own eyes and in the eyes of others. Biblically speaking, not a single use of the word *pride* is positive in Scripture, and pride has led more people astray than any other thing, including Satan.

You combat pride with humility. Humility is not, however, an abasing of self nor a loathing of self. Humility is not even a lessening of self. For all such actions requires you to still concentrate on self, which is still a form of pride. Humility does not mean you think you are small, that you are worthless, or that you are unworthy, for all such thoughts still focus on your ego and self. Don't misunderstand; before God, you are unworthy and you are small, and you may come to recognize that fact at some point in your life, son. In the Bible, those who did recognize their insignificance before God usually had their ego crushed when they came into the presence of the Lord. But each time, God had to get them to stop looking at themselves and to focus on Him. Humility focuses on lifting up *someone else*—not on putting yourself down. Any focus on yourself is not an act of humility.

The Bible tells us to humble ourselves. How? By submitting to the hand of the Lord.[63] Your focus should be on God and lifting Him up. John the Baptist said of Christ, "He must increase, but I must decrease."[64] This can only be done when you lift up Christ instead of yourself. When you focus on someone else, you will be lifting them up in your eyes, which naturally means you will be lessening yourself.

Lifting up others includes people around you as much as it does to God. Peter went on to explain, "Yea, all of you be subject one to another, and be clothed with humility: for God resisteth the proud, and giveth grace to the humble."[65] When we submit to others, we are putting them before ourselves, which is how we can be clothed with humility.

Humility requires you to get your eyes off yourself and on to someone else, to exalt that person, to lift him up, to give him praise, to set him first. That is the essence of humility, which is one of the reasons why humility is so difficult to truly achieve.

Son, pride takes many forms. It can be subtle or blatantly obvious in your life. It can pop up at any time your ego is threatened. Humility is much harder to achieve, for it requires you to take your focus off yourself and put it on someone else. It will be a constant battle to do this.

Job went through several stages of pride. The Bible says that he was upright when his problems began happening.[66] In an ash heap and surrounded by supposed friends, he begins to argue that

---

[63] 1 Peter 5:6.
[64] John 3:30.
[65] 1 Peter 5:5.
[66] Job 1:1.

his calamities were unjust—that God was being unfair.[67] Job's focus was on himself. He was in the throes and iron grip of pride and his ego. God then came in and crushed Job's ego.[68] Despite that, Job wasn't willing yet to let go of himself and submit totally to God. He still had a remnant of his ego left that he tried to resurrect. He said of himself, "Behold, I am vile; what shall I answer thee? I will lay mine hand upon my mouth."[69]

God still didn't have Job's focus correct, so He continued to smash Job's ego through two more chapters.[70] In the end, Job was completely crushed. He said, "Wherefore I abhor myself, and repent in dust and ashes."[71] But that still wasn't enough for God. God wouldn't turn Job's calamities until Job got his focus right. He then gave Job an interesting task. He told him to pray for his three friends—the three God was already angry with.

In fact, God did not turn Job's captivity *until* he prayed for his friends.[72] Job needed to repent of his pride and then focus on others. Once he did that, God blessed him. God lifted him up. Son, we spend way too much time trying to lift up ourselves, but if we lift up someone else, God will bless us for it.

Sometimes our egos will have to be utterly crushed in order for us to finally get our eyes off ourselves. This is the act of *being* humbled. Trust me, son, it is better if you humble yourself by moving your focus onto others rather than having God humble you by systematically demolishing your ego.

---

[67] Job 23:2-7.
[68] Job 38:1-40:2.
[69] Job 40:4.
[70] Job 40-41.
[71] Job 42:6.
[72] Job 42:10.

# Beaten by Girls

To swell my pride and the image I had of myself, I was good at sports. Being one of the best at something builds that ego, and I had a fairly high opinion of myself in these areas. In track, I was fast and rarely lost a race, and being beaten by a girl was inconceivable. No way was I going to be beat by a girl.

For a time, I ran track, specializing in the 100-meter dash and the 400-meter dash. My dad signed me up for a Jesse Owen's track meet and entered me in the 400. When I got to the starting line, a somewhat chubby kid in the lane next to me gave me a grin and said, "Well, so much for this race."

Wondering why he was even in the race to begin with, I asked, "What do you mean?"

He nodded past me. "See her? She always wins."

I turned to look. In the first lane was a tall, lanky girl perhaps two years older than me. Under other circumstances, I would have looked at her differently, but because she was in a race with me, I saw her as nothing more than competition—but with a slight distinction. Because she was a girl, I felt compelled beyond the norm to beat her and to prove that no girl was faster or better than Greg Baker. No sir!

I looked back at the chubby kid. "Not today," I told him.

He shrugged. "She always wins," he repeated.

Grinding my teeth, I fixed my gaze ahead. *Not today.*

I was in the third lane of the race, so I was starting on the track curve slightly ahead of the only girl in the race. When the gun sounded the start of the race, I took off. After about ten steps, the chubby kid waved at me as I burned by him and shouted, "Go get her!" I noticed he was already pulling up to a slow jog. I still didn't know why he was in the race.

I ran my heart out. I was absolutely determined to beat this girl. My ego did not want to take the blow of having to admit that some girl beat me in a footrace. I prided myself on the fact that no girl *had* ever beaten me. No need to start today.

I never saw her the whole race. Since I was in the third lane, assuming she was running the same speed as I, she would not draw abreast of me until we came into the final stretch, but when I hit that last straightaway, I was still in the lead. I had this! I ran so hard that my legs began to grow numb. I took in great gulps of air to keep those legs pumping, and just maybe ten yards from the finish line, I grew curious. I wanted to see how much of a lead I had. I wanted to know by how much I was crushing this girl who "always wins." So I turned my head to look.

At that precise moment, she caught up to me. Fear struck through my heart as I realized how close she was. I wobbled, straightened, and then lunged for the finish line. I crashed across the line, stumbled, and fell, rolling over and over. I came to a stop some distance beyond and lay there gasping desperately.

My stomach felt nauseous. I'd never run so hard in my life. I tried to hold it back, but then my stomach rebelled, and I had to stumble over to the grass where I emptied the contents of my stomach. I hurt everywhere, but I still didn't know whether or not I'd won.

When the times were announced, I discovered to my utter horror that I'd lost by 1/100th of a second. I was stunned. I'd lost! My legs couldn't hold me up any more, so I collapsed into a sitting position on the track edge, still in disbelief.

I'd lost to a girl.

Then the girl had the gall to come over to me, still looking fresh and full of energy, and said, "Good race. It's been a long time since someone actually gave me a run for my money."

I responded with an ungracious grunt.

I got my silver medal, but I had to stand below that girl while she received her gold one. I've never forgotten how that loss struck hard at my pride. I was a very unhappy person, and *almost* winning didn't matter. I'd lost, but the fact that I'd lost to a girl rankled the most. It just wasn't right. The natural order of things had been upended, and the image I held of myself had taken a serious blow.

So is the nature of pride.

Years later, I sat across a chessboard from another girl named Jane during a high school chess tournament. We'd been paired because our rankings were similar. I'd just started playing for our chess team in my sophomore year, but I was much stronger than my ranking indicated. I felt confident I could beat her, and again, my pride would accept nothing less. It just wasn't right to be beaten by a girl, and having already tasted such a defeat in that track meet, I wasn't about to let it happen again.

I played white, so I opened up with a standard e4 pawn opening. Jane countered with e5, so I elected to try the Danish Gambit and see what she was made of. She quickly fell for a trap, and I had her on the ropes. I ran her king out in front of her pawns, exposing her to a ruthless and unrelenting attack that should net me a checkmate in a short of amount of time.

So confident was I that I became careless. I saw an opening to capture more material and further isolate her king, and I jumped on it, putting my queen on a square in what I assumed was a dominate move. The moment I took my hand off the piece and hit the chess clock that began her move, I realized my error. I'd hung my queen, meaning she could take it for free without any loss of material or position.

My heart dropped into my stomach as Jane studied the position and then carefully, probably fearing some trap, took my queen and pushed the knob on her side of the clock. I couldn't believe I'd given her a significant advantage when the game was mine to win. I got angry—angry at having made such a blunder, but more so because I had now given this girl a wonderful opportunity to defeat me. That thought was intolerable!

I made my next move, slamming the piece down on the board and then smashing the clock knob. I gave her a scowl that clearly indicated my displeasure. She could feel it too. My attitude practically bled off me. She began to shrink down in her chair, and her moves became more and more timid, which suited me just fine. Maybe she'd make a similar blunder to mine.

I continued to play, being none too gentle with the pieces or the chess clock. At one point, I crafted an amazing trap that if she fell for would win me the game. But she saw it and got out of it. My frustration must've been so intimidating to her that she didn't win the game until she'd cornered my king with four queens—way more than what was necessary.

In a timid voice, Jane said, "Good game," and half offered her hand for me to shake.

No. I'd been beaten by a girl. My pride, anger, and bruised ego would not suffer such a humiliation lightly. I stood up, ignored her hand, and stormed off.

Again, such is the nature of pride.

# The Height of Indignity

During a trip to California, my mother took my brother and me to the beach to play in the ocean. Dad had to work, so he wasn't with us on this particular trip. When we arrived at the beach, I took my swimming clothes and headed toward the men's restroom to change. My mom stopped me.

"Greg, I can't watch you in there," she told me. "You'll have to change in the girl's restroom."

My mother was nervous about all the strangers, and since I was only a boy of around eight or so, she didn't want me to be anywhere where she couldn't easily get to me. But even at that age, my pride rebelled against that idea. The problem was that changing in the girl's restroom might be okay for my little brother, but in my mind, I was a big boy and didn't need this overzealous oversight.

"But Mom!" I protested. "That's the girl's bathroom. I'm *not* a girl!"

"I know that. But I think you'll be safer this way."

My little mind turned rapidly. I just couldn't imagine going into the girl's bathroom. *It's just not right,* my mind screamed. "I won't take long, Mom. I'll be real quick."

"Gregory Scott Baker, you'll do as I say, or you won't go swimming."

Her response wasn't fair. Mothers shouldn't be able to use your full name as ultimatums. I decided to try one more time. "Mom—"

Her head cocked to the side, and I knew I was on the verge of pushing her too far. I gave in.

But walking into the girl's bathroom behind my mother was the height of indignity, let me tell you. I was a boy. I didn't belong there. Good night, I didn't even want to *be* there. The few women standing before sinks and mirrors didn't seem to mind, but I was fuming and very embarrassed about being in there. I don't think I've ever changed so fast in my entire life. I just wanted out of there.

This instance left an undeniable impression on my mind. Even young boys have egos and an image of themselves they wish to uphold. Pride is not an adult problem. It infects us at the youngest ages.

## Fainting in the Desert

Pride is also not an affliction solely of the young. It can absolutely crop up at any age and can lead to sin or just plain foolishness. Such was the case I found myself in one day on a hike at the mature age of 39. I wanted to take my four boys, Dalen, Kyle, Owen, and Jacen on a hike up into the Superstition Mountains to see Weaver's Needle. Getting caught up in some work, I did not properly plan ahead, and all I ate before our hike was a nice, healthy, nutritious bowl of Frosted Flakes. Yeah.

We took the dog, Jax, along with us and started up the mountain to a saddle where we could get a good view of the Needle. The climb was 2.5 miles one way and rose about 1500 feet, and my boys took to the trail like mountain goats. The only thing slowing them down was their huffing and puffing dad. It certainly wasn't the dog.

Still, I was determined not to let my kids show me up. I trudged ahead doggedly, keeping up a steady pace on the rocky trail and refusing to let my boys get too far ahead of me. The sun was high and beat down on us unmercifully—though it hardly seemed to matter to the boys. I felt its touch keenly, and sweat drenched my shirt underneath my backpack. Still, I refused to give in as my boys continued to hop and skip around the trail as if born to it.

About three quarters of the way up, I finally called a break. The world had begun to spin a little bit, and despite my pride, I realized that if I didn't take a break, I'd be in pretty rough shape. We stopped on the edge of the ravine where there was a convenient flat rock for me to lean up against. I flopped against it more than leaned, trying desperately to get my breath. My boys, meanwhile, had found a much larger rock they could climb to see sweeping views of the canyon we had been hiking up. *Good for them.*

"Just give me a moment, boys," I said. I leaned against the rock, still gasping, and closed my eyes to keep the world from spinning too much.

After a bit, it slowly dawned on me that something was wrong. I twisted around and idly wondered why there were rocks in my bed. Sharp rocks bit into my back, neck and hands. I reached over to wake my wife to ask her, but felt oddly lethargic.

A voice, seemingly to come down through a long tunnel, asked, "Dad, are you okay?"

I shifted in my bed again, trying to move the rocks. I was really uncomfortable. Someone shook me.

"Dad? Are you okay?"

I knew that voice. That was Dalen, my son. But what was he doing in my bedroom? I forced my eyes to open. Sunlight stabbed at me, and I winced. *What?* I saw the face of my very concerned son leaning over me. *What?*

Then it all came back to me in a rush. I was on a hike—not in my bed. I looked around and realized I was no longer leaning against the rock slab, but was now lying amidst the rocks on the trail. I had passed out and rolled right off that rock and fell among the other rocks. Not good.

I pushed myself up to a sitting position, feeling faintly embarrassed. I'd actually fainted. I've never done anything like that before, ever. I had pushed myself too hard in a vain attempt to keep up with my more energetic boys. I had let my pride push me into an act of foolishness. First, I should have eaten better. Second, I should've taken my time and had more breaks.

In a situation like that, most people would probably just go back. Not me. We still hadn't made it to our goal yet, and I didn't want to let my kids down. I ate some food, waited until the dizziness had passed, and then pushed on. Admittedly, I did it at a much slower pace and took more breaks, but this second decision of mine was still rather foolish. I hadn't trained my boys as to what to do if something had befallen me, so who knows what might have happened if I'd fainted again.

I didn't, and I made it back down safely, but much later, upon reflecting back, I realized how foolish the whole hike had been. I had nothing to prove to anyone, but I had an image in my head of what I needed to be for me and my kids, and I pushed myself beyond reason to keep that image. Such is the essence of pride. My ego and pride caused me to do something incredibly foolish that could have turned out significantly worse than it did.

Thank God for His grace and mercy. But, son, pride will need to be combated for the rest of your life. One of the hardest things next to defeating your pride is first recognizing your pride.

# CHAPTER SIXTEEN

# Giving and Keeping Your Word

Commitment is a lost concept in our culture. Rare is the man who will commit himself to something and then do everything within his power to see that such a commitment is kept. When I was pastoring, I would hear over and over, "I don't want to promise." In other words, they didn't want to commit. Son, when you give your word to do something, you are committing yourself to do it.

You have perhaps heard the phrase, "My word is my bond." This should still be true of you, son. Not only should you keep your word if you give it, but you should be willing to give your word. A real man is someone who can give his word, is not afraid to commit himself to something, and then will do everything in his power to meet his commitments. He doesn't shirk from responsibility. He doesn't avoid situations that might be difficult or uncomfortable. He isn't afraid to commit himself.

One of the reasons I trust the Bible is because I believe that God will keep His promises.[73] But understand what this belief means. God has committed Himself to doing certain things, thus

---

[73] 2 Peter 3:9.

His word has bound Him to a course of action as securely as a prisoner is bound in jail. God is a willing prisoner of His own Word. He cannot break His promises. He cannot go back on His commitments. God didn't have to make these promises. He didn't have to commit Himself. He didn't need to bind Himself. The fact that He did so gives me strong confidence in the Lord.

Son, what sort of confidence do people have in you? Are you bound by your word as surely as God is? Are you a man who can be relied upon? Are you a man who is willing to commit himself?

Commitment is an attitude, a determination to see something through, to bind yourself to a particular course of action. A marriage, for example, is a commitment. If you find a girl willing to enter that sacred institute with you, then keep your vows. Commit yourself wholly to the marriage. More than that, commit yourself to her. Some men commit themselves to the marriage, but not to their wives. They won't get a divorce, but they treat their wives in an unmanly manner. If you are committed to your wife, son, you will have a good marriage.

This doesn't mean you shouldn't be wise about what you commit yourself to. In the Bible, Jephthah made a vow that cost him his own daughter.[74] Many think he made the vow foolishly, and perhaps he did. No promise should be given lightly, and many things should be considered carefully before you commit yourself,[75] but the fear of committing yourself wrongly should not be the excuse to never give your word at all.

Weak men cannot commit themselves because they cannot keep their word. Son, do not be among them. Learn to commit

---

[74] Judges 11:34-40.
[75] Ecclesiastes 5:4-5.

yourself to those things that are worthy of your word, and then keep your promises.

## "Show Up, or You're Fired!"

While attending Bible college, I had made a commitment that I would not miss Sunday services because I had to work. I refused to work a job that required me to work on Sunday. This decision was based on a conviction I had and a commitment I had made. Since I was training to be a pastor, I didn't think it wise to miss church even for work, and I figured God would provide me the right job so that I wouldn't have to work on Sundays. Would you believe it? For my entire life, I've never had to work a job that required me to come in on Sundays...with one exception.

For about three years, I worked at a place called United Global Nippon (UGN). At one point in my time with them, the company landed a lucrative contract, and we suddenly found ourselves overwhelmed with work. In a very short amount of time, the leadership began instituting mandatory Saturdays for all shift personnel. Since I worked second shift, this scheduling wasn't that big of a deal, so I was able to get most of my Saturday ministry duties done before I had to go in to work.

But the work kept coming, and soon we were called into a shift meeting one Friday. The shift supervisor said, "I got word from on high that we have to start working Sundays for a short time."

The complaints and grumbling from the employees hit him like a wave. He glared at us. "This is the way it's going to be. Anyone who doesn't show up will be fired! Stop your whining. The pay will be double time."

That announcement perked up everyone. We'd get double our normal pay for working on Sunday, and yes, that was enticing. Back then, I was making nearly thirteen dollars an hour, and for working on Sunday, I would be getting nearly twenty-six dollars each hour. Not bad for a college student in the late 1990s.

"No questions?" he asked. It really wasn't a question. "Good. You're dismissed."

I caught up with him right outside the break room. "Sir, I won't be in on Sunday."

He fixed me with an angry scowl. "Greg, I've already covered this. If you don't come in, you're fired."

I shrugged. "I guess I'll be fired then." I didn't say it with any heat. I didn't show any anger. I didn't show any remorse. I made it as matter of fact as possible. I explained, "I made a commitment years ago that I would not miss church, even for work. This is a promise I made to God. I intend to keep it. If that means you'll fire me, then so be it."

I worked that day. I worked on Saturday. But come Sunday, I didn't go in. I didn't even call in. I figured he already knew I wasn't going to be there. All day long I wondered if I had a job come Monday. When Monday rolled around, I went to work like normal. No one said a word to me. I worked that day, and every day after until Friday. On Friday, we had another shift meeting.

The supervisor said, "We've got to work Sundays again. Everyone is required to be here. It is mandatory."

I raised my hand.

With a disgusted look, the supervisor waved his hand at me as if brushing me aside. "I know. I know. You won't be here."

No one even complained that everyone else had to be there except me—perhaps double-time pay made up for it in their minds. I never did get fired, and I never had to work on Sundays. I had made a promise, and I intended to keep my promise even if it cost me my job. When I agreed to work for UGN, it was with the understanding that I would not have to work Sundays. I'd never committed to working for them on Sundays, but I had committed to church.

God worked it out, but son, even if I had been fired, keeping my word is much more important than any job. My integrity is not something that can be bought with double pay. Let me ask you, is your integrity cheap or cheaply bought? Would you have compromised?

## Into the Den of Booze

During the early years of pastoring, a couple began attending our church. The man was a recovering alcoholic, who had actually spent over $10,000 in two months on alcohol earlier in the year. That admission sort of rocked me. I couldn't even imagine that. I've never in my life tasted any sort of alcohol except what is contained in Nyquil. Spending that much money on booze absolutely floored me.

Anyway, this man had made a commitment to his wife that he would stop drinking. He also made the same promise to me. But one Sunday night after evening church, I got a call from this man's wife.

"He hasn't been home all day," she said. Her voice was rock-solid, emotionless.

I suspected she'd insulated herself from her husband's frequent infractions. In her mind, she wasn't one bit surprised that her husband hadn't kept his word. "I'm sorry to hear that," I said, trying to be the sympathizing pastor. I did feel bad for her, and I was somewhat angry that this man had gone back on his word to me.

"I think I know where he's at," she continued. Her voice dropped a bit, and I could tell she was really troubled by all this, despite her attempt at being the tough wife of an alcoholic. "Can you go get him?"

Both my eyebrows shot up. "Get him?"

"Yes. I'm sorry, Pastor. I don't want to do it, but I'm afraid he won't come home, and he'll spend all our money. Can you?"

I didn't want to—not because I didn't care about her or her husband, but because I didn't know that world. The only other time I'd ever been in a bar was during college when my roommate and I went into a bar to preach a sermon as part of an assignment for preaching class. We went in, got bemused permission to preach, and preached two short five-minute sermons to the four men sitting at the bar. They seemed to like it and even invited us back next week as the banged their beer mugs on the bar in approval. That experience was surreal. Despite that invitation, we never did go back.

So walking into a bar by myself was not something I wanted to do. But I had made a commitment to be a pastor and that meant sometimes I would need to reach into the miry pit of sin to try to help someone. "Okay," I agreed. "Where do you think he's at?"

She told me, and I got in my car and drove over to the bar. The bar was small, part of a tiny strip mall off a street near the Evans cemetery. That location seemed somehow appropriate. Half hoping he wasn't in there, I stepped through the bar door.

I was still dressed in my Sunday clothes—suit, tie, and dress shoes. As a sort of buffer, I carried my Bible in with me. I looked around, still hoping I wouldn't see him, but there he was, sitting in front of a short bar, his back to me. He was slouched over, his hand curled around a mug half filled with what I supposed was beer.

Three other men besides the bartender were in the place, seated together off to one side at a table. They took one look at me and knew instantly that I didn't belong. They began making mocking remarks as I walked past. One said, "Daddy's here," and giggled. I had no idea what he meant. I was a chaplain for the Weld County Sheriff's office, and I had a badge with me. I thought seriously of flashing it and saying, "Federal Marshall! Everyone out!" just to see what would happen. I didn't. Oh well.

I walked up behind my church member and just stood there. A mirror covered the wall behind the bar, so I could see his face when I stepped up. He was looking down, however, his jaw somewhat slack and his eyes glazed. I just stood there, not saying a word. I heard more comments from the other patrons, but I ignored them. I waited.

Eventually, my church member picked up the mug to take a drink. When he did, he lifted his eyes and saw me in the mirror. I've never seen someone turn ghost white before, but he did. Seeing his pastor standing behind him must've felt like seeing an avenging angel. He might have expected to see his wife, but seeing his pastor there? Well, I may have very well scared him sober.

He nearly dropped the mug and half spun around, no doubt wondering if he wasn't seeing things. "Pastor?"

I nodded. "Yes."

"What are you doing here?"

"Your wife sent me to fetch you home." That set the other men off in a fit of laughter. I ignored them all. "Come on. Let's go."

Obediently, he slipped out of his stool and followed me outside. I wanted to say all sorts of things—and sitting in my car, I did give him an earful. I was disappointed in him for not keeping his word, and trust me, I had a lot of work to do if I was going to help him salvage his marriage and get him to have anything to do with his children.

He broke his word, and it cost him. On my part, I had made a commitment to him and his wife as one of my church members and that meant loving him no matter what—even if it meant pulling him out of a bar. It was a promise I'd made—one I needed to keep.

Son, a commitment is no small matter. The depth of your character is revealed when you can make commitments, and the depth of your manhood is revealed when you keep your word.

# CHAPTER SEVENTEEN
# Work Hard, Son!

Work should not be a dirty four-letter word. Nothing is wrong with play, and much play often requires effort. The defining distinction between work and play is not that one is fun and the other is not; rather, work involves building, creating, or producing, and play expends effort without any truly useful or tangible byproduct—it is only entertainment. In other words, work gives but play takes. When you play, you are taking the enjoyment and pleasure of the effort, but you are not creating anything beyond that. Work finds enjoyment and pleasure in producing something that enhances an environment or contributes to a greater whole.

Nothing is wrong with play, but work is the key to your future, son. The apostle Paul gave himself little credit for anything, except in one area. He said, "But I laboured more abundantly than they all."[76] Paul worked harder than anyone else, so he accomplished more. Paul created something everlasting, and through his effort, gave us a foundation in the New Testament,

---

[76] 1 Corinthians 15:10.

through Christ, that has enriched every single Christian down through the ages.

There are essentially three principles of work:

1. Work hard
2. Do the work right
3. Enjoy the work

Solomon explained that while our bodies have breath we should work hard.[77] You cannot take anything to the grave, but you can leave something behind. Your legacy will always be found in your work and what you leave behind for others.

But whatever work you do, work hard at it. Give it your full effort. Don't do a halfhearted, slipshod job. A man works hard. He doesn't need to be reminded to work. He doesn't need to be told to work. He doesn't need motivation to work, for the work itself is motivating enough. Sloppiness is a sign of laziness, pure and simple. Son, if you are sloppy in your work, you are being lazy; and laziness should have no part in your character.

Of all the negative qualities a man could have and of all the sins in which a man could indulge, laziness is among the top three worst. I wouldn't give two cents worth for a lazy man. Without fail, laziness has caused more grief to others than anything else. In fact, some of the most heinous sins committed against people are likely a direct result of laziness.

The following is a short list of common qualities of a lazy man:

---

[77] Ecclesiastes 9:10.

1. He complains
2. He is angry
3. He is resistant
4. He makes frequent excuses
5. He justifies inaction
6. He is unfaithful
7. He scorns others
8. He is shortsighted
9. He plays the victim

And when you work, do the job right. Don't cut corners. Make it the best you can do, and if you are able to do better, then do better—even if that means starting over. People will remember your work more than anything else about you. Your work will be a lasting monument to who you are as a person, son, so do the job right. If you are sent to clean your room, clean it. Do it right. Don't stuff everything under the bed or in the closet. Take ownership of your room.

Taking ownership of the job is what a man does. A man sees to it that the job is done right. People can tell a lot about you by how hard you work and if you do everything in your power to do the job right. Homework, son, is work. It is your job, so do it right. Do it to the best of your ability.

Then learn to enjoy work. Tremendous pleasure comes in accomplishment, in creating, in producing. Unexplainable joy comes from doing a job right and knowing it is done right. A joy comes with knowing you produced something that matters. Son, it is the closet you'll ever get to the divine quality of creation. Work is creation. It is accomplishment. It is the path of success.

It is true that you will not enjoy all aspects of a job, but you can take pleasure in doing it right. Few things in life will give you more satisfaction than work.

Son, learn to work and learn to love it.

## Hunting Giant Rodents

I'm of the belief that shooting animals should not be done simply for sport. If you shoot it, then you should eat it. The only three exceptions to that rule is self-defense, population control, or you are exterminating a pest that threatens livestock, land, or an ecosystem. Still, there is no doubt that hunting itself is a sport, and it can be an enjoyable one.

But more than a sport, hunting has traditionally been a necessary job. Pioneers hunted for meat to feed their families as an example. Today, we hunt primarily for sport, not survival. But like many things, if you want to succeed at it, you must put in the work. Sports can be used to teach life lessons. To succeed at a sport, you need to work at it. We all enjoy winning, but few enjoy the punishing practices, drills, and workouts that prepare you to win.

I must've been around fourteen when my dad, Pastor Jenkins, and I went on a javelina hunt. A javelina is an oversized rodent, not actually a pig, although they certainly look more like a pig than they do a giant rat. We traveled north out of Mesa, Arizona, to a section of Sycamore Creek where Pastor Jenkins was confident that we could flush out some of these 40-pound mammals.

I stepped out of my dad's truck and looked around. Being February, the creek had water in it, but the sun was already beating down on us, and I felt unusually hot for that time of the year. I wasn't all that enthusiastic about tramping around in the desert in the heat, carrying a rifle and other hunting gear, but if I were going to bag one of those critters, it looked like we were going to have to do some walking.

A tall, steep mountain lay immediately in our path to the south. A sharp ridge shot out of the mountain and ran toward the east. Pastor Jenkins pointed to the top of the ridge. "Javelina like to bed down in narrow ravines. I bet we'll find some on the other side."

Pastor Jenkins was a large man in his fifties. I noted sourly that the only weapon he carried was a sidearm. "Where's your rifle?" I asked, knowing that he was going to suggest that we walk to the top of the ridge.

He patted the weapon strapped to his side. "I'll hunt with this."

He didn't put me at ease. I half wondered if he were along just to see if I could shoot something. He didn't seem to be taking this hunt very seriously. Oh well.

Pastor again pointed to the ridgeline. "Let's get to the top. We'll be able to scout the land better from up there."

My dad nodded. "Sounds good. Let's go." My father carried a rife that had the stock modified so he could reach the trigger with his shorter arms. I carried a youth .243 Winchester, perfect for what we were going to do. Still, I had to lug the thing to the top of the mountain.

We started up, and we made it about a third of the way, weaving around cactus and other desert plant life, when my shoulder started to throb. For whatever reason, my nerves lay close to my skin atop my shoulders. Carrying anything there, backpack or rifle, invariably caused my shoulders to feel pinched. Yes, it hurt, so I constantly shifted the rifle from one shoulder to the other or just carried it in both hands for a time to give my shoulders a break.

The sun rose in the sky, and the heat rose with it. By the time we reached the top of the ridge, I was sweating, hot, uncomfortable, and not having a bit of fun. This was too much like work for my taste! The other side fell away toward a narrow ravine at the bottom. Thick brush and a few isolated trees choked the ravine bed and sides.

"They're probably bedded down at the bottom," Pastor Jenkins commented. "You two go ahead on down. I'll stay up here to see what I can spot."

Just what I thought. *He is along to see if I can shoot something. Figures.*

"Come on, Greg," Dad said, beginning a careful descent down the slope. "You go about halfway down, and I'll get in the bottom of the ravine. Keep your eyes open. If there are any javelina down here, I'll flush them out ahead of me. You might get a good shot if you're patient."

I eyed the brush choked ravine bottom. "Okay," I said, relived I didn't have to tramp through all that.

Pastor Jenkins stayed on top, I went about halfway down, and my dad navigated the very bottom of the ravine. In this way, we swept the entire ridge from top to bottom. Once my dad made it to the bottom, I could hear him making noise as he shoved his way through the brush. Figuring that any javelinas down there would run out ahead of my dad, I pushed ahead of him and began to drop down lower to the ravine. And then I heard them.

On the opposite side of the ravine, between two trees, a game trail cut up sharply from the ravine bottom. Three javelina ran up that path and disappeared farther up. I stopped, dropped to one knee and raised my rifle, putting the scope between the two trees. Then I waited, figuring that game trail to be the most likely escape route for any more javelina in the bottom of the ravine.

My heart started pounding as adrenalin rushed through my system. The moment I'd wanted had come. This was why I'd come on this hunt. Taking game was the whole purpose of hunting, so this was the big moment. My hands started to shake, and I shifted to rest my elbow on my knee.

Sure enough, a small javelina darted up the path, but I held my fire. If I were going to shoot, I wanted to shoot something bigger than that one! Then a good-sized javelina darted up the path. I put my crosshairs on its nose and jerked the trigger. You're supposed to squeeze the trigger, but I was too excited. I jerked the trigger, and the gun went off. I don't remember the sound. I just remember the recoil moving my scope sights, but I could have sworn I saw that critter topple over and fall into the ravine. But it happened so fast, I wasn't sure.

Still shaking and with my heart still pounding, I stood to my feet. "Dad!" I yelled. "I think I got one!"

Dad didn't respond. I looked back in his direction, realizing that I had gotten ahead of him and was torn about finding him or going to look for my kill. Then BOOM! I ducked and fell on my face among the rocks. Dad was shooting, and I was in front of him!

BOOM! BOOM!

I stayed down, scared that I was somehow in the line of fire. The echoes dissipated down the ravine, and after a moment, I looked up. "Dad?" I yelled again.

"Yeah!" he replied from somewhere behind me and at the bottom of the ravine.

"Did you get one?"

"Yeah!"

"Me too!"

"Good!"

I still couldn't see him. "Are you done shooting?"

"Yeah!"

What I didn't know at the time was that my shot had turned several of the javelina around, and they had charged right at my dad. My dad only had a split second to react and started shooting. It took three shots, but he managed to bring one down and scare the others away.

I got up and scrambled down the slope to the bottom of the ridge. I wanted to be certain I'd actually gotten one. After a moment, I found it, lying on its side at the bottom of the ravine. The shot had been perfect, taking it right in the chest behind the shoulder.

But that's when the work really began. With Pastor Jenkins and my dad giving me advice, I gutted the animal and cleaned it. The sun still beat down on us, and flies buzzed excitedly around me as the smell of blood drew them to us in droves. There wasn't even a hint of a breeze to relieve the stifling heat that gathered at the bottom of the ridge.

After finishing that part of the task, not one I enjoyed all that much, we still needed to pack out both carcasses. I looked up apprehensively at the ridge. "Do we have to go back up there?" I asked.

Dad shook his head. "This ravine comes out near the creek. We'll go that way and follow the creek around to the trucks."

Though his plan sounded better, it also meant our trek was technically further. Still, that beat having to lug a 40-pound animal to the top of the steep ridge. Regardless, the walk out was agony! I carried my critter for a time. Pastor Jenkins had tied the legs together and made a sling of sorts so that it could be carried over one shoulder. With my shoulders already hurting, this added weight didn't help it. My shoulders throbbed unmercifully as we navigated the bottom of the ravine.

By the time we got out of the ravine and to the creek, I felt like I was going to die. I let the beast down, stumbled to the creek, and filled my hat full of water. I then dumped it over my head. That felt so good!

My poor dad was in worse shape than I. Heat exhaustion had set in. His face looked both red and pale at the same time, and he looked to be dizzy. We still had some ways to go, and the heat and sun were unbearable. It was way too hot for February! Pastor Jenkins volunteered to carry the animals, and I got stuck with the rest of the gear, including my dad's, which meant I had to carry both rifles. Well, at least there would be a measure of balance.

We started off. No more than five minutes later, I was completely dry from my dunking. So I stopped again to dump a hat full of water on my head and stagger on. The walk seemed to take forever. We became strung out with Pastor Jenkins in the lead, marching resolutely on with a javelina slung over each shoulder. I came next, about thirty yards back, trying to keep upright and put one foot in front of the other. This was work— and all to kill a giant rodent, the meat of which was not really all that tasty to begin with. My father brought up the rear, walking with his head bowed and a determined look on his face as he tried to keep from being overwhelmed from heat exhaustion.

But we all had it to do, and complaining about it would not make any difference at all. So we plowed on, the only comfort I found was bathing my head in creek water every five minutes or so. My shoulders were on fire from the rifle straps pinching my nerves, every step was one of agony, and I knew I'd end up sunburned. My canteen was empty, and my dad had warned me about drinking the creek water, so my mouth was parched and my tongue felt too big in my mouth.

Eventually, we made it back, and I never saw such a welcoming sight as the truck sitting under a tree near the creek. My dad caught me smiling about an hour later as we drove along the highway toward home. "What are you smiling about?" he asked.

"Just thinking of the hunt. I got 'em!"

"You sure did. We both did."

Honestly, we put in way more work than those critters were worth, but that wasn't the point. With all the work I put into getting him, I was very much proud of myself. Ours wasn't an easy hunt. That hunt cost me something, so it made the accomplishment so much better.

That is the nature of work, son. If it costs you something, you appreciate it to a degree you never would unless you put the work into it. Work makes everything more valuable.

## "Quit or You're Fired!"

My first job as a Bible college student didn't last very long. I worked at a place called Americall, a telemarketing firm with employees who called people and tried to sell them a product over the phone. I needed a job, so I left Arizona early to go to Indiana and get a job before college started. Dr. Row, one of the college professors, put my cousin and me up in his house until the dorms opened and the semester started.

Dr. Row either took me down to Americall to do an interview or he found me a ride. I got the job, but I'm telling you, I didn't like it, and so I admit I didn't put the work into it that I should've. Each person was assigned a booth and a headset. Calls were automatically routed to you if someone picked up and answered the auto dialing program. I had to try to get these strangers to sign up for a credit card they no doubt didn't need.

My job required me to give the pitch and then at least two rebuttals if the person was resistant. I also had a quota I had to fill each week of "sales." I was amazed at how easily some people made their sales. I struggled to get anyone to sign up, but some of my fellow coworkers breezed through sales as if they were manna dropped from heaven.

Part of the problem was that I didn't like the work, and because I didn't like the work, I was not giving my best to the job. I would pray for calls to be routed to someone else, and when I did get a call, I didn't come through as confident or interested.

It all came to a head one day when I took a call made to a very nice man. He listened patiently and quietly to my entire speech. He didn't interrupt one time. He asked no questions until the end. When I wound down, hoping I'd get him to sign up for the credit card, he asked a single question, "Would you get this?"

That answer set me back on my heels. *Would I?* I didn't really believe in the product myself. I had no interest in a credit card at that time in my life or the inherent dangers that come with it. So I responded, "No. I wouldn't."

"Thank you for your honesty," he said, and hung up.

I sat there for a moment trying to determine if I'd done the right thing when my supervisor seemed to pop up from nowhere. "Greg," he said, his face stern, "follow me."

I had a sinking feeling in the pit of my stomach. I got up and followed him to the conference room. He beckoned me to a seat. "I was listening to that call," he informed me.

I knew what that meant. He wasn't happy with the way I'd handled that customer. I tried to take the high road. "But it was the truth. You can't expect me to lie, do you?"

"No. But that's still a problem. If you don't believe in what we're doing, you shouldn't work here. In a way, you are lying to every customer you talk to. If you aren't on board with what we want, then you aren't part of our team." He leaned forward. "You've made it clear how you feel, so you have a choice. You can quit or I can fire you. Take your pick."

I just stared at him, dumbfounded. He continued to wait for my answer, so I finally said, "I guess I quit."

"Very well. I'll get the paperwork ready. Wait here."

He walked out leaving me alone in the conference room. He was right. If I were to do the job, then I needed to do it right. That company didn't need someone on their team who wasn't going to give his best and work on their behalf. I focused on the nature of the work and took displeasure in it, but what I should've done was find pleasure from doing the best I could do. I didn't do my best. I didn't even try to do well. I betrayed the trust of the company that had hired me, I tried to excuse my actions, and I mentally complained about the work. I didn't deserve to work there or deserve to get a paycheck from them.

Son, it's amazing how much bad luck lazy people have and how much good luck hard-working people have. Perhaps it has nothing to do with luck and everything to do with their character.

# CHAPTER EIGHTEEN
# What You Say Matters

Son, everything you say and the way you say it matters. Words are very spiritual. They are the essence of thought, for without words, thoughts cannot be expressed or conveyed to another. What we say is so important that I even wrote an entire book on the subject called *Fitly Spoken*. Suffice it to say, every word you use matters. The Bible says, "A word fitly spoken is like apples of gold in pictures of silver."[78] So strongly does God feel about the words we speak that Jesus said, "Every idle word that men shall speak, they shall give account thereof in the day of judgment."[79]

Words matter. Each word you say can have a significant impact on another's spirit, mind, and emotions. And it is not just the words you say that matter, but also the tone in which they are said and your body language you use while saying it. All say something to the listener. It matters if you hurt someone with your words—and it doesn't matter if you didn't mean to do so. You are

---

[78] Proverbs 25:11.
[79] Matthew 12:36.

still responsible for not only what you say, but how you say it and how the other person takes it.

So many relationship problems occur because of misunderstandings. Son, please understand that life is relationships. God meant for the majority of your earthly happiness to be derived from your relationships. Words are the essence of how we connect with these relationships. So the more careful you are with your words, the more careful you are with your relationships.

I find it disheartening when teenagers use negative words so cavalierly with each other. I find it distressing every time I've had to counsel a marriage, and the focus of their anger was based on the words they said to each other. We speak rashly and harshly, not realizing the full impact our words have on the spirits of others. A wise man learns to mitigate his words and watch his tongue.

The Scriptures teach that we are to be swift to hear and slow to speak.[80] We are also warned that the tongue can't be tamed.[81] If the latter is true, then we must be on constant guard against our tongue. We can't trust it to say the right thing without thinking. We must be diligent to put limits on our tongue, to bridle it so that we can keep it under control, never trusting it because it can't be tamed.

No one is perfect in this area, but son, a man of integrity seeks to understand the impact his words have on others. Words are powerful tools that can do an incredible amount of good, but they can also destroy lives. But the right type of man will be constantly vigilant against the words that come out of his mouth.

---

[80] James 1:19.
[81] James 3:8.

I should warn you that silence *is* saying something. I know that silence is golden, and I know that people have told you to say nothing if you have nothing good to say. They are correct, but not always. Silence is better than saying the wrong thing, but silence can also be taken as saying something. There are times when silence is the wrong thing to do. Imagine if Jesus had remained silent when He found men cheating worshipers at the temple.[82] Imagine if Jesus had remained silent when the disciples refused to allow the children to come to Him.[83] But then Jesus knew when to remain silent too. While being accused, Jesus refused to say anything in His own defense.[84]

Words convey meaning, attitude, intention, and ideas. Words are powerful. I'd dare say that the mastery of words and when to use them is the greatest skill any man could ever learn. Nothing in the realm of relationships, and I mean that wholeheartedly, can compare to the power of the words we say.[85] Of all the disciplines a man could study and master, the discipline of the tongue is the greatest. A man who can control his tongue can easily master any other discipline.

Son, how careful are you with the words you say?

## "You Didn't Ask"

In college, during a time when I didn't have my own transportation but was relying upon the generosity of others, I needed to find a ride to meet my mother who had come from Arizona for a visit. She was staying at someone's house in

---

[82] Matthew 21:13.
[83] Mark 10:14.
[84] Matthew 26:62-63.
[85] James 3:2.

Munster, Indiana, and I was to meet her after work one day. I needed a ride, so I approached one of my fellow college students.

"I need a ride," I said. "My mother's in town. Are you going by way of Munster?" In my mind, I was asking for a ride. I figured he was well within his rights to say no if he wanted to, and I never considered the fact that he would take my words all wrong.

He agreed to take me, but on the way there, he was unusually silent. When we pulled up to the house where my mother was staying, he said, "I didn't appreciate the way you did that."

I froze in the act of opening the door. "What?"

"You never asked me for a ride," he said, his face intent and a bit angry. "You practically ordered me to give you a ride."

"I asked you," I said puzzled. "You said yes."

"You told me you needed a ride. You never said, 'Can I have a ride please?' You just assumed I would do it."

I wanted to argue with him at first. I didn't understand why this was bothering him so much, but I realized that I hadn't actually asked. I hadn't expressed any grace, courtesy, or empathy for his efforts in doing me a favor. Perhaps in his shoes I would feel the same way. I had begun learning that you can't deal with people from the perspective of what you believed to be true, but you had to approach them from what they believed to be true. Otherwise, we'd just end up in an argument. I didn't want an argument, and I didn't want to destroy my chance of getting a ride from him in the future.

"You're right," I said, feeling as if each word was an admission of defeat and guilt that I didn't feel was justified. "I'm very sorry. You went out of your way, and I was being unkind. I'm sorry." Then feeling I needed to add a bit more so that he wouldn't feel I was just saying that without meaning it, I added, "Thank you for bringing it to my attention too. I needed to hear it. So thank you for both the ride and the words."

He nodded shortly. "You're welcome."

We parted amicably, and I learned a powerful lesson. The words I said and the way I had said them had rubbed him the wrong way. Upsetting a classmate certainly wasn't my intention. In honest truth, I was just anxious to see my mother whom I'd not seen in some time. He misread the situation and took it as arrogance, but it didn't matter. Since he saw it that way, that was the way I had to deal with it. If I told him his thinking was wrong, he'd just go away angry and possibly bitter. I'd accomplish nothing by challenging his perspective. But by using words that dealt with his understanding, I was able to retain a friend.

Son, your words matter. Every last one of them.

## The Great Teaser

I'm a great teaser. I express many of my emotions toward people by teasing them. Teasing is both a strength and a weakness. In fact, I've said before that I only tease people I like. There is truth in that. If I am comfortable around a person and feel we have a strong relationship, I will invariably begin to tease them with my dry wit and humor. Unfortunately, I've hurt quite a few people over the years with the words I've spoken in jest.

I remember one case while pastoring. We had a man in our church to whom I'd grown close. He was a much older man, but he understood the role of pastoring so we had similar perspectives on the ministry. Because I'd grown close to him, I would, without thinking, tease him.

He actually loved it, but his wife did not. His wife was a tremendously insecure woman who bordered on paranoia. She read many things into everything, even to the point of accusing her husband of having affairs with women a third of his age. I knew all the people involved and I knew it to be completely groundless. But his wife would take every little thing and blow it way out of proportion.

Despite that, she was a good woman who did the best she could with her particular paranoia. She came to see me one day, and without any preamble at all, said, "If you want us to leave, just say so."

I was dumbfounded. Not only did I not want them to leave our church, her husband was one of my closest friends. I had absolutely no idea what she was talking about. "I don't want you to leave," I said, struggling to understand.

"You clearly hate my husband," she said. "If you are trying to run him out, why don't you just come out and say so?"

"I don't hate your husband. He's one of my closest friends. Why would you think that?"

"You're always insulting him, always making fun of him. You do it all the time and in public."

Oh. I realized she was referring to my teasing. She was right. I did do it a lot and probably way too much. Because of how my dad's arms were, my dad would grow up either being very bitter at life or ending up with an outrageous sense of humor. My dad got the humor, and so I grew up where teasing was an expression of love. Insults were frequently tossed around in my home, but they were a way to express our love for each other. We never tiptoed around my dad's deformity. He could laugh at himself, so I learned to do that as well. In fact, I once had a man hurling insults at me, and I just assumed he was teasing. So I laughed along with him and teased him right back. Not until later did I realize he was deadly serious. Trust me, patching that relationship up took some finesse.

With this woman, her insecurities had left her so sensitive to words that she took my teasing as direct and deliberate insults. Her husband understood and would tease me right back, which I always enjoyed. We had a great relationship. But I had to deal with her from her perspective. I had to somehow assure her that I didn't hate her husband—or her.

Convincing her that I loved them both required many, many more words of assurance. Son, understand that one word of injury may require a hundred words of healing to undo. And it doesn't matter if someone simply misunderstands. Once the injury is done, it exists, and must be addressed.

## Tricked into Getting a Blessing

Words have power, and how we use them can change how people behave and even interact. A fellow college student, John, offered to give me a ride so I could get a haircut. I needed one pretty bad, and he apparently didn't have anything better to do.

"I'll give you some gas money," I told him by way of thanks.

John waved his hand. "No need. I'm happy to take you."

I took out five dollars. "Here, take it."

"Nope. And you can't make me take it either."

I grinned at him. "We'll see."

John returned my grin. "Come on. Your haircut awaits."

He drove me down to the barber shop, and I got my haircut. On the way back to the college, I used a puzzled tone of voice to say, "John, I have a question. If someone wanted to be a blessing to me, should I accept the blessing even if I don't need it?"

John frowned. "What do you mean?"

"Doing something for someone else is important on two fronts, right? I mean it might be good for the person who receives the blessing, but it is also good for the person giving the blessing, right? If I refused his kindness, wouldn't I be robbing him of a blessing too?"

He thought about it for a moment. "I think so. The Bible says it is better to give than to receive, but if you didn't receive it, then there would be nothing given either. Everyone loses."

"I agree." I took out the five dollars. "Then I need you to take this five dollars, John. I want to give it, but if you don't take it, you'll be robbing me of a blessing."

He stared at me long and hard. Finally, he snatched the five dollars out of my hand with a chuckle. "You win. Not fair using my own words against me!"

I laughed. "Told you I could get you to take the money."

My words had the power to get John to completely change his mind about accepting the money. Words convey intent and ideas, which in turn produce response and change. The right word said at the right time can change a life. The wrong word said at the wrong time can injure and even destroy a life.

Son, words are power. Just look at what God did to create the universe. He *spoke* it into existence.[86] Words define understanding, intent and action. Let's use our words carefully.

---

[86] Genesis 1; John 1.

# CHAPTER NINETEEN
# The Root of All Evil

Other than your tongue, your attitude toward money might be the second greatest indicator of the state of your character and pride. The Bible says that the "love of money is the root of all evil: which while some coveted after, they have erred from the faith, and pierced themselves through with many sorrows."[87] The coveting of money has caused many men to err from the faith and to toss aside their integrity and character. And you, son, will be no exception unless you can get a handle on your attitude toward money.

Money is important to us because it can provide us with the things of this life. It can keep us fed, sheltered, and clothed. It can buy us convenience and fun. Money can even buy a "sense" of security and is one of the reasons why Jesus said that it is easier for a camel to pass through the eye of needle than for a rich man to come to Christ.[88] A rich man relies on his money to meet his needs, so in his mind, he has no need of Jesus Christ.

---

[87] 1 Timothy 6:10.
[88] Matthew 19:24; Mark 10:25; Luke 18:25.

Nothing is wrong with being rich. The mistake, son, is *trying* to be rich. Nothing is wrong with money. The mistake is *loving* money. For the love of money creates attitudes and desires that lead you into being the sort of son of whom few fathers could be proud.

Son, you need to learn how to handle money correctly. You need to understand the value of money, learn to budget, learn to save, learn to pay your debts, learn to give, learn to be generous, and learn about good investments. But more than all of that, you must learn not to allow money to capture your heart. Your character and integrity should come before money. You should never compromise your character for money, and you should never be so stingy with money that you can't give as the Lord directs.

Don't let money own your heart. Understand the role that money plays in your life and be wise about it. God uses money as a benchmark to determine if you can be trusted with the true riches of life.[89] There are things much more important than money and things that money cannot buy, such as a good marriage, loving children, true friends, a walk with God, joy, peace, and becoming a good man. In order to give you some of these true riches, God may look at how you handle money.

The way you spend money is the way you spend your life. If you work a job, son, for one hour and you get paid ten dollars for your work, then how you spend that ten dollars is how you will spend one hour of your life. That money represents your life, so how you spend your money is also how you spend your life. God

---

[89] Luke 16:11-13.

looks at that to determine what is important to you. After all, where your treasure is there will your heart be also.[90]

Your attitude toward money and how you use it is an indicator of your heart and your character. Show me what you spend your money on, and I'll find out what is important to you. Think about it. If you tell one girl you like her, but spend more money on a different girl, then where is your heart really? Which girl will think you really like her? If you tell God that you love Him, but you spend all your money on games, then where will God think your heart lies?

There should be a balance when it comes to money. You shouldn't be so stingy that you hoard it all for your own wants and desires. You also shouldn't be so careless that you spend it on anything and everything that takes your fancy and interest. How you spend your money should be done with wisdom and prayer. Control your money; don't let it control you. Greed and covetousness should have no place in the heart of a man.

## Refusing a Pay Raise

About three months before I was to leave and begin pastoring in Colorado, the company where I was employed had yearly reviews. I was asked to meet with the supervisor for mine.

"Sit down, Greg," he told me when I came in.

I plopped down in the seat in front of his desk.

"Do you understand how this works?" he asked me.

I nodded. "Based on my performance, you'll offer me a per hour raise in quarter increments up to a dollar."

---

[90] Matthew 6:21; Luke 12:34.

"Correct." He took out a folder with my name on it and opened it. "You've been a very good employee, and we like your work ethic." He went on, pointing out a place or two where I could improve. He then talked about the vision and direction of the company for a bit before getting down to business. "Based on your review, we're going to give you a dollar raise per hour." He then looked at me expectantly, no doubt thinking I'd be excited by this announcement. Few employees had a yearly review good enough to net a dollar an hour raise.

Indeed, it would be the most money I'd ever made up to that point in my life. At that stage of my life it would more than meet my needs. However, within three months, I would be quitting and heading out to Colorado to begin pastoring. At the time, I had a "scholarship" of $20,000 to help me get a church started. The money from the raise, in my opinion, would simply be a distraction. I didn't want to be lured away by the money. I'd heard of other Bible college students who had found great jobs in the secular work force, and the appeal and desire for money lured them away from their dreams of pastoring or being a missionary.

In and of itself, nothing was wrong with the money or working the job I worked, but I didn't want the temptation. So I shrugged and said, "I don't want it. I'd like to turn down the raise and keep working at my current pay rate."

My supervisor's jaw dropped. "You what?"

"I don't want it. In fact, I don't need it. So I'd like to turn it down."

He fumbled with his folder before leaning back in his chair. "In all the time I've been here, you are the first to ever turn down a raise. Why?"

"I'm quitting in three months anyway. It's no secret that I am heading to Colorado to pastor a church. I don't need the raise to pay my current bills, and I don't want the distraction or the possibility that the money will tie me down here."

"You could save it," he suggested.

"Sure I could. The problem is having it."

"I don't understand."

"I've just noticed that when you have excess money, there is a temptation to spend it. To increase your lifestyle. When I go to pastor, I don't want to step backward because the income won't be there initially. I could save it, but I just don't want to deal with the temptation right now."

Honestly, I wasn't being spiritual. I was being practical. I just didn't want to be tempted from doing what I wanted to do— pastoring a church.

"I don't know, Greg. No one's ever turned down a raise before. I'm not sure what to do. Let me talk to some people."

"Sure."

I got up and left. Outside, some of my coworkers cornered me, knowing I'd just had my yearly review. "How did it go?" one asked.

"Fine."

"Well?" another demanded. "How much did you get?"

There was a bit of competition here and internal comparison. "They offered me a dollar raise, but I turned it down."

All three of them stopped and stared at me. "You did what?" one demanded, aghast that anyone would do such an absurd thing.

"I told them I didn't need it."

Another snorted in disgust. "You could've given it to me then!"

"Or me!" the third chimed in.

I laughed. "Sorry."

About two days later, my supervisor called me back into his office. He had a slightly bemused expression on his face. "Well, Greg, you sure stirred up a hornet's nest when you turned down that raise. I ran your choice up the chain of command, and it actually went all the way to the CEO for a policy decision. No one has ever turned down a raise before." He shook his head in wonder. "The decision is that you can't turn it down."

I blinked, startled. "You're going to *make* me take a raise?"

"That's about the size of it. There is a fear of litigation if you don't take it." He waved a hand in front of his face. "I don't pretend to understand it all. Anyway, you're getting the raise whether or not you like it."

Money is powerful, son. Never let it get a grip on your heart. Even the company's decision to force me to take the raise was a fear of litigation and the financial impact such litigation would have. You don't have to turn down raises to prove that you aren't in the grip of money. I only made that decision because I was leaving in three months anyway. Even as young as I was, I understood the power of money and how easily it can capture a man's heart.

## God Provides

When I took the church in Greeley, Colorado, the first immediate effect was that I forfeited $20,000 of a fund that had been set up to help start brand new churches. Gospel Light Baptist

Church of Greeley, Colorado, was not a brand-new church. It was about two or three years old. The previous pastor had resigned, leaving only a single family as part of the church when I took it over.

The church had been renting a little storefront building, and the owner of the property told me, "I knew the other guy, but I don't know you. You have two months and then I want you out." So I had to go find another building. In my opinion, I did everything a person would do to start a church, but that didn't matter. Because the church was already in existence, I forfeited the $20,000.

What I found out was that God will provide anyway. For starters, when I first moved into the city, my wife and I stayed with some other college graduate and his wife while looking for a place to live. I really, really didn't want to move into an apartment. My last experience hadn't gone so well. So we began looking at trailer parks. At least we would have a yard separating us from our nearest neighbors instead of a wall.

We found a little 12x60 trailer for sale for $10,000. The price seemed reasonable. The place was a mess, however. The carpet smelled. It needed a thorough cleaning. The walls had holes in them. But hey, the payment was cheap, and we were young without any kids, so I figured I could clean it up. What's more, it would be ours. We'd still have to pay lot rent, but that plus the loan payments would be cheaper than any apartment rent.

The dealership was willing to finance the trailer, but we'd have to come up with $500 as a down payment. That wasn't really a problem. I had a cashier's check for a bit over $2,000, so all I needed to do was get it cashed.

Not thinking this would be an issue, my wife and I went to the drive thru of the first bank we could find. I put the check in the little tube carrier and sent it over to the teller. After a moment, I heard a buzz and then a voice through the speaker. "You're wanting to cash this check?"

"Yes."

"Do you have an account with us?"

"No. I just need to cash that check."

"We can't cash a check this large without an account."

The answer puzzled me. "Why not? It's a cashier's check. It's just as good as cash."

"There has been a lot of cashier's check fraud, so our policy is not to cash such a large amount without an account first."

"Then can I open an account?"

"Absolutely."

"Let's do that then."

"Hold on." He did something and then asked, "What's your address."

I hesitated. "I don't have an address yet," I told him. "That's why I need the check cashed. Once I do that, I'll be able to get a loan and then buy a trailer. That's when I'll have an address."

"I'm sorry, sir, but we need an address in order to open an account for you."

"So you're telling me that in order for me to get this check cashed, I've got to have an account with you, but to get that account, I have to have an address?"

"Yes."

"But to get that address, I need to cash this check first!"

"I'm sorry, sir."

Irritated, I got my check back and went to the next bank. I heard the same story. My wife and I went to about six banks that morning looking for someone who could open an account and cash that check. Each time, we were told basically the same story. On the seventh bank or thereabouts, I just walked in and gave a little speech. The bank was called Norwest.

"Look," I told the innocent girl behind the teller, "I need to cash this check. No, I don't have an account with you. Yes, I would like to open an account with you. No, I don't have an address yet because I have to cash this check first so that I can get an address. Can you help or not?" I was probably a little short and rude, being so irritated.

Without changing expressions, she said, "Wait here."

She left to go talk to someone. When she came back, she said, "Our vice president is here. Maybe she can help you."

Finally! I'd be able to talk to someone with the power to do something. I met with the lady and explained my situation. She nodded in sympathy. "Okay. We're a national bank, so we can use an established address from back in Indiana to open your account. Unfortunately, it will take about two or three days before the funds will be available in your account."

I didn't like hearing that. "I need at least $500 right now though."

She considered it. "I might be able to help. But why do you need the money?" I told her. "Let us try to get the loan for you," she offered after hearing me out. "I think we can get you a much better interest rate and save you from having to put $500 down."

That I liked hearing. Without a paycheck, I needed all the money I could get right then. "The situation is a bit time sensitive," I told her. "I need an answer by tomorrow."

"We can do that."

I then opened an account, deposited my cashier's check, and then filled out a loan application for $10,000.

That day, I fasted and prayed. All night, in fact, I prayed, asking God to do a miracle. We needed a place to live, and this was the best deal I'd been able to find so far. I needed this to work. The interest rate from Norwest was significantly better than from the other lender, and if I didn't have to give up that $500, all the better. If at all possible, this is what I wanted.

I got a phone call about noon the following day. I'd fasted and prayed up to this point. I was very hopeful. The loan officer said, "I've got good news and bad news. The good news is we approved your loan."

I smiled, feeling relieved. "Then what could be the bad news?"

"The loan is only approved for $7,000."

"What? What happened?"

"With your current credit rating and the value of the trailer, this is all that we can do."

I told her I'd have to think about it. I hung up completely dejected. All that praying, all that fasting...for what? I couldn't believe it. Where was God? Then the phone rang. Absently, I picked it up, still feeling sick to my stomach. "Yes?"

"I'm looking to speak to Greg Baker," a man with a Spanish accent said.

"That's me."

"You called about my trailer two days ago?"

I'd called a lot of people that day. "Probably. Which one is it?"

"We listed it for $14,000."

I remembered. It was a larger trailer, 14x74, with three bedrooms and two baths. The one I was trying to get had only two bedrooms and one bath. But $14,000 was still more money than I could afford at the time. I opened my mouth to tell him that when he said, "I'm willing to sell it for $7,000."

My words got all tangled up in my mouth. When I got them straightened out, I asked, "Why did the price go down?"

"Long story. My brother and I bought this as an investment. He cheated me and disappeared. All I want is my money back. Do you want to come see it?"

I did. "We'll be right over!"

This other trailer was in much better condition than the one we were trying to buy. It was bigger, had more space, and the lot rent was even cheaper. And it was in my price range—exactly in my price range. We sealed the deal and bought this other trailer instead.

If you study the flow of this story, you will see how none it couldn't have happened unless several things had first gone wrong. God provided. At the end of two years of being in Greeley, I pulled out a little journal of blessings I'd kept and calculated that the Lord, above and beyond any salary I received, had directly or indirectly provided $40,000 to help me get settled and start a church. That was twice the amount of what I'd forfeited that was to have been given to me over the same period.

Son, when money doesn't own your heart, then God has no problem providing the financial support you need—as long as He has your heart.

# CHAPTER TWENTY
## Get Your Own Stories

Perhaps one of the best pieces of advice I can give you, son, is to get your own stories. Regardless of where you live or what your circumstances are, nothing can substitute for being engaged in life. Here in the United States, we live in an entertainment-driven society, which means we experience things vicariously more than we do directly. We sit too much in a chair watching others live life instead of living life ourselves. Watching television and movies, playing video games, and enjoying sporting events where we are spectators is not living life. It is merely watching someone else do it.

Don't misunderstand. I'm not saying that any of those things are intrinsically bad or evil, but the most powerful memories and experiences in your life will be those in which you participate, not watch. My fear is that we have trained ourselves to fear life in some sort of subtle way. We don't want to take risks for fear of being hurt. We don't want to experience success because of the hard work involved. We don't want to volunteer for new responsibilities for fear of failure.

Son, don't be that way. Opportunity breeds opportunity. If you want to get the most out of life, you will need to walk through the doors that God opens for you. This doesn't mean you walk through every door. Satan is just as capable of opening doors for you, and you need wisdom to discern the difference. But those opportunities that God gives you should be jumped on. We don't create our own stories because we are too busy watching someone else's—real or fiction.

You have to put yourself out there. Life is relationships, and if you want to experience life, you will have to become involved with people. You will need to work with people. You will need to strive with people. You will need to bond with people and do things. Pain might be involved. You might get hurt. You might fail. You might look bad in the eyes of others. But each experience adds to your character and manhood. Each failure or success grows you in ways you cannot anticipate.

Son, don't miss out on life because you are more comfortable watching someone else's life. God will give you opportunity, and when you take that opportunity, even greater opportunity comes. My thirteen years of pastoring were not wasted. Starting a church was both difficult, painful, and terrifying at times, but incredibly worth every drop of sweat, blood, and tears spilled in its pursuit. The memories and relationships I gained from the experience has enriched me beyond belief.

Imagine if Peter, James, and John hadn't given up their fishing business to follow Christ. What would they have missed out on? What would've happened if David hadn't offered to fight Goliath? What would have Peter learned if he had not stepped out of the boat to walk on the water to Jesus? Imagine if Abraham had not left his homeland and obeyed God. What would the Bible be like if Paul and Barnabas hadn't left Antioch to begin their first missionary journey? Would there be a book of Daniel if Daniel hadn't refused to eat of the king's meat? What would Jesus' ministry have been like if John the Baptist hadn't defied an entire nation to preach the coming Messiah? The list goes on and on.

We know these biblical stories because the people involved took the opportunities God placed before them. They lived their lives. Son, I'd rather *live* life than *watch* life.

## A Miserably Wonderful Hunt

I like hunting, and I don't like hunting. I love the wilderness. I love nature. But I am not that enthusiastic about the cold, field dressing a kill, or hauling a kill up and down mountains. My father and I had gotten drawn for an elk hunt when I was fourteen. I was keen on missing school—that part I liked—but I wasn't so interested in sitting around in the late November cold, high in the mountains of northern Arizona on the off chance that an elk would wander in front of my rifle scope.

The first day of our hunt was miserable—at least to me. I hate cold. I was desert bred, and this pine forest, high in the mountains had no resemblance to the warm climate I was used to. We staked out a game trail that first day, and all I did was shake and shiver. I began to regret being there, and all I wanted was for the hunt to be over so I could get into the truck and turn the heater on full blast. To top it off, we saw nothing. Not even a squirrel so much as made his furry snout known to us.

I became grumpy and miserable company. I complained, balked, and daydreamed about being home where I could read a book or play a computer game. My dad picked up on my attitude as I was not really trying to hide it and became irritated. He didn't show it much, but he did give me a lecture about it later that night.

The next day, much too early for sane people to be getting up, we drove out to where we were to hunt again. But this time, I had an idea. The day before, while sitting there in the cold, I kept hearing shots from other hunters off in one particular direction. Someone was finding something to shoot at, so I determined to walk off in that direction and see if I could find an elk that would stand still long enough for me to put a bullet into him.

"I'm going that way," I told my dad, pointing to a line of cedar trees beyond what we called a knockdown area—a place where many of the trees had either been cut or knocked down to promote new growth.

Dad looked at me, no doubt wondering if I were just going to walk that way until he was out of sight, circle back, and climb into the truck. But he decided to let me venture out alone. "Okay," he said. He nodded in another direction. "I'll be off that way."

Sounded good to me. I walked across the break toward the cedar line, thinking that if the sun didn't come up soon and warm things up significantly, I would indeed circle back and climb into the truck. The blowing wind didn't help my attitude much, but at least I was determined. This was my idea, and I at least intended to see it through—for the moment.

I reached the cedars and walked into them. I figured to use the cedar trees as camouflage. About fifty yards farther on, the cedar line came to an end and before me was another one of those knockdown areas. I could see for a goodly way there, so I figured I'd walked far enough. I found a nice stump and sat down to wait for the sun to come fully up.

I must've sat there for about an hour, trying to warm my stiff and freezing body. I kept shifting positions, trying to fir something comfortable and wondering why people actu thought this was fun. Then I heard a sound. I snapped my eye my heart thumping in my chest, and the cold fleeing my lir if I'd been plunged into a hot spring. That sound was made by a large animal.

I stood slowly to my feet so I could peer around, and then I saw a line of elk walking toward me. Now my heart began to race. I could hear it thumping loudly against my rib cage. I couldn't believe it. Elk! I knew that the bull elk always trail behind the cows, so since my tag was only for bull elk, I'd have to wait for that line of elk to pass me. I lifted my little .243 Winchester and sighted through the scope, looking at each animal as it crossed my crosshairs to see if it if it wore any antlers.

But then that lead cow got a whiff of me. She stopped, lifted her nose in the air, and sniffed. The rest of the elk froze in place. My line of sight ran up a gentle slope perhaps twenty or thirty feet tall. I couldn't see over it, so only the front six animals were visible to me. The rest stood on the other side.

Soon my arms began to shake trying to hold that rifle up. I felt unusually warm suddenly and began to sweat, and that's when out of the corner of my eye, I spotted another line of elk converging on me from my left. I swallowed. I had to do something. I couldn't continue to hold the rifle up like this, not with my skinny arms, so I began to slowly pivot about to see if there was a bull elk visible among the other group.

I spooked them. They saw me move, and both columns turned and bolted. I grunted in disgust. I'd blown it, but something in me didn't want to let it go so easily. I lowered my rife and took off running after them. There is really no way I could catch them, but I ran anyway, just as fast as I could over the rough terrain. When I topped the small hill, lo and behold, a single four-point bull elk (we only count points on one side of the antler rack in the west) was trotting parallel to my position.

I jerked up my rifle, but when I did, I accidently breathed on the scope. Since I'd been running, my hot breath fogged that scope right up. I put my eye to the scope and saw only fog. I pulled back and looked at the fogged-up scope in disbelief. I then looked up at the elk as it trotted around a tree and disappeared. My chance was gone.

Perhaps I should've been angry, but maybe because I wasn't cold anymore, the escapade struck me as humorous. I'd just run after a herd of elk! I chuckled and carefully cleaned my scope. When I looked up, a spike bull elk ran into view. He wasn't as big or pretty as the one I'd just missed, but he was a bull elk and the tag said I could shoot and eat him if I wanted.

I wanted.

Careful not to cloud up my scope again, I lifted my rifle and took aim. That elk sensed me, I guess, for it took off running full tilt. I placed my crosshairs on its nose and squeezed the trigger. The animal disappeared all at once, almost as if it had never been there. For one terrible moment, I wondered if I'd been seeing things. I couldn't be absolutely sure the elk I'd just shot at actually had antlers.

Fearing I'd shot a cow elk by mistake, I took off running again to the place where I'd last seen it. There, I found my elk. Yes, it did have antlers, but no it was not yet dead. My bullet had taken it through the neck and severed the spinal column. It was paralyzed from the neck down. Feeling triumphant, I pulled out my sidearm, intending to put the animal out of its misery.

Unfortunately, my sidearm was a nine-round .22 revolver. I didn't know better, so I took aim right between the eyes, figuring a head shot would end the elk's suffering. I shot nine times into its forehead, but without any visible effect. The animal's skull bone was so thick and hard that the bullets just ricocheted off.

I didn't know what to do. I hadn't been able to kill it! Should I shoot it again with my rifle? I was still debating that when the animal finally died of its own accord. Then came the hard work. I had to field dress the animal and then somehow pack it back to Pastor Jenkin's pickup truck. I looked around, but couldn't see my father or Pastor Jenkins anywhere.

I was loath to leave my kill unattended, so I pulled out my knife and began the process of gutting the elk alone. Before long, I was stripped down to my t-shirt and had blood all the way up past my elbows. My dad and Pastor Jenkins finally found me and helped me finish the process. We then managed to drive the pickup truck to the spot of the kill, loaded the elk onto the truck bed, and returned to camp where we skinned it.

I had completed my first successful hunt. The experience changed me. I realized that if I'd given up because of the cold, I'd never been able to complete the hunt. The meat we got from that elk was tender and juicy. I remember eating it with pride. I'm glad I ventured out there, took a bit of risk, and dealt with the cold and wind. I'm glad I got to make that memory.

## King of the Raft

When I was in grade school, I attended Camp Ironwood, a Christian camp in California, for several years in a row. One particular year, they had a raft chained to the middle of our swimming lake. It wasn't long before we got the idea to play King of the Raft. The game was simple: get on and throw everyone else off.

But on this particular day, two adult counselors decided to take over the raft. When I arrived, they were standing on the raft and casually picking boys out of the water and tossing them willy-nilly out into the lake.

One of my friends saw it. "Not me," he said as one kid did a spectacular belly flop. He winced. "Nope. I'm not going over there."

"Come on," I urged. "We can take them." I always loved being the underdog, so this challenge appealed to me.

"I can watch just fine from here," he said.

He wasn't budging, so I swam out to join about eight other boys circling the raft and trying to find some way to get on and push off the adult counselors. I decided there was no time like the present. I swam up to the edge, slithered up like a seal, and charged the nearest adult. He whirled, snatched me off my feet and spun me out over the lake. I landed on my back, my arms and legs all askew. That hit stung! I couldn't see it, but I would've laid a wager that my back looked all red from that slap. It was like a reverse belly flop.

I swam back, trying to think it through. None of us was strong enough to get the counselors off the raft. We would need to work together. We tried a few things, and we all got tossed off again. I realized we all had one major flaw in our thinking. Our goal was wrong. We were trying to become king by pushing off the counselors and remaining on ourselves. One or two of us, however, needed to probably go over the side with the counselors and let the rest take control of the raft.

I turned to one of the boys as we treaded water. "Look, I'll lock his knees together and then you push him off."

He gave me a puzzled look. "But won't you go off with him?"

"Of course, but you can help me back on. Once he's off, we can keep him off easier."

He grinned. "Let's do it."

I waited for an opening, slithered up on to the raft, and charged my targeted counselor. It worked! I wrapped my arms around his knees and held on for dear life. He bent down, trying to peel me off, but his balance was wrong, and when two or three other kids tackled him, he teetered and then toppled right off the raft. I went with him, but we'd done it! We got one of them off.

The raft was big enough that the remaining counselor couldn't protect the entire perimeter. It wasn't long before he too went over under a swarm of laughing and jeering boys.

We stood up there cheering and yelling, "Kings of the raft!" I happened to look over at my friend still standing on the shore. He waved, and I waved back. There was one big difference between us. I experienced the victory directly. He merely watched it. Yes, he wanted his fellow boys to conquer the counselors. He cheered for us. He wanted us to win! When we did, he was excited. Only he watched it, and I did it.

Son, don't watch others enjoying life. You do it. Get out there, find something to get involved in that is right, good, and holy, and do it. Opportunity breeds more opportunity.

# About the Author

Greg S. Baker was born in 1975 to a Christian couple. Reared in church all his life, he came to accept Jesus as his Saviour and attended a Bible college, graduating with a bachelor's degree in pastoral theology. He pastored a church in northern Colorado for thirteen years until God called  him to expand his writing ministry. He now resides in Arizona.

His writing passion pervades nearly every aspect of his life. As a child, he was an avid reader and fell in love with words and their ability to stir the imagination and convey ideas. Writing became a tool by which he conveyed his passion for his God and Saviour to the world around him. As a pastor, he used his love for writing to bring to others over twenty years of experience in the ministry, counseling marriages, and healing relationships.

He is married to the love of his life, Liberty, and has four incredible boys who alternately remind him of the excitement of youth and the inevitability of the passage of time. He loves to play sports, play chess, and tinker around with computers. Other than writing, he continues to pastor in various capacities and operates an editing business for Christian authors.

You can connect with Greg through his website GregSBaker.com. He loves hearing from people and engaging them as an active part of the writing process for his future books. If you love reading, then stop on by.

Made in United States
Orlando, FL
16 April 2022

16899034R00135